75
Years of
INDIAN FOREIGN POLICY

JOURNEY *of a* NATION

Years *of* INDIAN FOREIGN POLICY

War, Peace and a World Realigned

MADHAV DAS NALAPAT

RUPA

Published by
Rupa Publications India Pvt. Ltd 2022
161-B/4, Gulmohar House,
Yusuf Sarai Community Centre,
New Delhi 110049

Sales Centres:
Bengaluru Chennai
Hyderabad Kolkata Mumbai

P-ISBN: 978-93-5520-391-5
E-ISBN: 978-93-5520-407-3

Fourth impression 2026

10 9 8 7 6 5 4

Printed in India

Dedicated to my mother Kamala Das,
who never lost faith in her eldest son,
no matter how many others did.

Contents

Foreword

I do not take seriously the dictum *Vasudhaiva Kutumbakam* (the world is a family). The world has never been a family. It never will.

M.D. Nalapat's book *75 Years of Indian Foreign Policy: War, Peace and a World Realigned* is riveting, erudite and provocative. He does not shy away from candour and unequivocalness.

India, according to Nalapat, has been a soft power, which is on the road to becoming a hard power. Even today, India cannot be pushed around. The eight chapters critically address the complexities of foreign policy and diplomacy of the major powers: the United States of America (US), the People's Republic of China (PRC), the European Union (EU), India and Russia. Three decades ago, the United Nations (UN) would have found a prominent place in the book. Today, it is no longer taken seriously due to incidences like the time when President George Bush chose to attack Iraq, bypassing the United Nations Security Council's (UNSC) decision.

Prime Minister (PM) Jawaharlal Nehru was a great man but not a great foreign minister. Nalapat is rightly unsparing of Nehru's indefensible mishandling of our policy regarding Kashmir and China. Nehru should not have taken the Kashmir question to the UNSC, certainly not under Chapter VI of the UN Charter, which deals with disputes among member states. Nehru opted for Chapter VII, which is about aggression by one member state against another. In the UNSC, the Kashmir question became the India–Pakistan question.

Broadly speaking, Nehru misjudged the intention of Chairman Mao Zedong, who wanted to 'teach India a lesson.'[1] China's 1962 invasion hastened Nehru's death. To this day the Kashmir issue and the Sino-Indian border dispute remain unresolved.

Nalapat is aware of the difference between foreign policy and diplomacy. Foreign policy determines what it is that we should do while diplomacy determines how we should do it. Those involved in foreign policy know that some disputes have no resolutions. The author suggests that such disputes should be skilfully managed.

Nalapat does not only ask questions; he provides answers. This is a lucidly written book that is very timely. Nalapat's sound judgement and *Weltanschauung* (world view) stand out. The range and value of this book cannot be exaggerated.

K. Natwar Singh
Former Minister of External Affairs
July 2022
New Delhi

Introduction

Covid-19 sent the world into lockdown in 2020, Afghanistan returned to Taliban control in 2021 and the war between Ukraine and Russia, which threatens to upend global logistics chains and risk nuclear confrontation between the North Atlantic Treaty Organization (NATO) and Russia, commenced in 2022. These incidents, over the past three years, have revealed the fragile nature of the global situation. In economics, the assumption of ceteris paribus, which means other things remaining the same, is often used. What has been made clear by just these three events is that when something changes in an entity, a lot of changes take place in numerous other entities as well.

While much is made of 'soft power'—which collectively refers to the tools, such as cultural exchanges and public diplomacy initiatives to help shape behaviour, in a nation-state's arsenal that do not punish, reward or threaten other actors into preferred behaviour—what is often disregarded is that to be effective, soft power must be based on a strong foundation of 'hard power'—the tools which do serve as sticks and carrots in international relations, such as explicit promises of trade incentives and threats of economic sanctions or military action.[1] India's hard power has grown with an increase in its economic heft and kinetic capabilities, and it is not accidental that India's image has grown with it. Given the interdependence of other economies with India's in this modern reality and the impact of other countries on it, policy needs to walk on two legs—foreign and domestic. The two need to be in balance, as a lack of symmetry in objectives would lead to complications that affect national life. Foreign policy must promote the objectives of domestic policy, which would include economic growth, consequently improving living standards, rather than the other way around. Domestic as well as global opportunities need to be identified and seized, and in this process, foreign policy plays an indispensable role.

The defining motif of the foreign policy formulated by Nehru was to pursue cosmic goals, which led to attention getting diverted from more practical, achievable goals that would have better served the interests of the Indian people. For example, a policy like non-alignment ought not to have been treated as an objective by itself but solely as a means towards more concrete goals, such as increasing opportunities for citizens to resettle gainfully in other countries or ensuring that security and economic interests are not harmed by other countries. However, when the means replace the importance of the outcome, a country performs in a suboptimal fashion, as India did in comparison to countries like South Korea and Japan, which had been devastated by war in the 1940s, even more than India had been by colonial rule.

Nehru's policy of non-alignment indicated that India resisted a unipolar world order dominated by the US. This stance has provided a strong rationale for a policy of opposing efforts at creating a unipolar world dominated by the PRC. Although deniers of the reality of Cold War 2.0, mainly involving the US and China, are still many, they are steadily reducing their number. Like a single male lion seeking to displace the reigning king of the pride in the jungle, Beijing is clearly engaged in an effort to displace the US as the primary power in the world. As was the case between the Union of Soviet Socialist Republics (USSR) and the US, this is a contest that is systemic in nature and, therefore, ultimately existential. In such a contest, given the dense network of contacts between the US and India, the choice of partner for India is obvious—it should be the US, not the PRC. The ongoing situation offers an opportunity for India to leapfrog on the economic as well as geopolitical scale, much as China did during Cold War 1.0 by taking the side of the US against the USSR.

The partnership between India and the US was not nurtured and allowed to flourish in the past. In the 1950s, India was given the opportunity to be at the global high table, including in the matter of securing a permanent seat in the UNSC, which was passed over. The difference between the policies of the Indian National Congress (INC) and the Muslim League during World War I, where the League was on the Allied side while the INC remained ambivalent, carried over in the policies followed by India after the death of Sardar Vallabhbhai Patel in 1950. This led to the US going along with the United Kingdom (UK) in regarding India under the INC as a far less dependable partner for the West than Pakistan. Rather than assisting the people of Pakistan, the US flooded the country with weapons, thereby driving India towards the USSR for its own supplies.

What was needed in the 1950s was a foreign policy matrix that prioritized India's own development and national interest. Given the rampant poverty and income deficiency in India, it is difficult to argue that the policy followed met this standard. Regardless, where economic growth is concerned, it is reasonable to assume that better relations with the US, in particular, would have ensured far higher economic growth than strong ties with the USSR did, as can be seen from China's case. In the 1950s, India could have demonstrated the superiority of democracy over authoritarianism by being assisted to grow rapidly in contrast to China, which was faltering in economic performance until the 1980s and had an economy smaller than India's. However, by the 1980s, the PRC had joined hands with the US to derive the dividend for its support during Cold War 1.0. As a result, the Chinese economy was nearly five times larger than India's by 2010.[2]

The situation facing the world at present has given India another opportunity, which must be seized to be the driving force of foreign policy. India is a quintessential swing state, necessary for success in any strategy by the US and its allies to ensure that the Indo-Pacific is not dominated by the PRC. Therefore, in Cold War 2.0, India can achieve a dividend similar to what China had derived in Cold War 1.0. However, this needs clarity of objectives and skill in navigating geopolitical currents—qualities demonstrated by China in an earlier era. Unlike the past, the geopolitical opportunity provided to India by global events should not be missed again. Countries need to be evaluated in practical terms and treated accordingly. A productive foreign policy that will help actualize the potential dividends for India is necessary. What may appear to be hard choices for our nation's foreign policy now may, in actuality, be the best course of action for the future of the nation.

This book looks at the countries that have been, or will be, important for India and what needs to be done to ensure that potential synergies with these nations are harnessed. While the primary focus is on the major powers, including, of course, PRC, Russia and the US, other countries, too, are important—if not yet then after a policy reset. This book aims to provide a structure for a foreign policy that deals with conditions as they prevail, rather than what they were or ought to be. To be of value, foreign policy needs to be an applied construct rather than be analysed in a way that is independent of the ground realities within nations and between them. Such analyses are 'cosmic,' in the sense that they bear no resemblance to actual conditions, and are, therefore, of scant value. Goals like the pursuit of stability in Pakistan, and a relationship of trust and mutual benefit with China, are indeed laudable, if only they can be achieved. However, this book chooses to focus on what is possible and why and how such potential needs to be unlocked. A focus on practice rather than theory is presented in the pages that follow.

1

An Inheritance Systematically Drained of Substance

The leaders of the INC, who led the freedom movement against the British rule, overwhelmingly came from the legal profession. It was perhaps their training in formal attributes that motivated them to wisely insist that the bringing down of the Union Jack from the Viceregal Lodge did not mark the birth of two new countries (Hindustan and Pakistan), but simply the British-assisted breaking away of a part of what, in atlases of the period, was described as 'India'.[1] This meant that on 15 August 1947, the succeeding government inherited the rights and privileges that had been enjoyed by the British Raj. Just as the British moved from Calcutta to Delhi to affirm themselves as the successors of past empires that had been headquartered in Delhi, so too did those who, with somewhat un-Gandhian alacrity, took over the offices and residences of the departing British officials. They saw themselves as the inheritors of a legacy of governance that stretched back two centuries—not two millennia—as ought to have been the case. The problem was that over the final 15 years of British rule, the British colonial office, Whitehall, had prepared for the colonial exit by draining away much of the substance of this inheritance. This was mostly by design but also, in part, because of the lack of confidence of the British in getting continued support from India under the INC's leadership after Independence. The control of the imperial government across the east, west and north of the country had been far greater in 1932 than when the Empire bequeathed the nation to its INC successors in 1947.

MOVING AWAY FROM PAST GOVERNANCE

There have been instances in history when the governance system of a country has moved radically away from its past because of a foundational change in the regime. For example, take the Meiji Restoration in Japan, or the post-war transformation of the ancient country from 1945 onwards. After its defeat against the US, shock ensured that the Japanese civilization and people adapted to democracy after centuries of undiluted authoritarianism. Another example of a change in a country's governance system is China after its 1949 makeover into the PRC by the Chinese Communist Party (CCP), led by Mao. Another such change included China's internal shift from stifling state control over the economy to a much more flexible economic construct that gave individual enterprises much more freedom from state oversight and control. This shift was facilitated by the denudation of the sharply conservative higher ranks of the CCP due to the Great Proletarian Cultural Revolution, coupled with the survival and ascent of Deng Xiaoping. Similarly, the shift from tsarist to Bolshevik Russia in 1917 saw comprehensive changes in the nature of the regime. So too, was the move from the Weimar Republic and its successors to National Socialist Germany in 1933.

In India, the changes caused by the exit of the British were much smaller—while the polity changed, the administrative and overall state mechanisms underwent limited changes. The political changes that took place permeated almost all the elements of society and certainly affected the direction of India's governance structure. While the former British colony and its princely surrogates did transform into the Republic of India on 15 August 1947, a substantial portion of the elements of this system, which were to be replaced, were retained and mostly still are in place. One such colonial element that was retained includes the broad mechanism of the three estates of the governance structure in India—legislature, executive and judiciary.

BREAKING UP A POTENTIAL SUPERPOWER

Ancient wisdom teaches us that it is better to aim for the stars and miss than aim for the moon and hit it. However, after 1947, over and over again, India's central planners did not even *aim* for the moon but for outcomes far less ambitious. History awaits an honest appraisal of the degree of success (and failure) of the individuals who took charge of what was left of India after Partition, when compared to the development in much of the rest of Asia, especially the east. Even before Partition, Myanmar, Sri Lanka and other territories were separated from the control of New Delhi since the British officials in Whitehall may have had a premonition that it was only a matter of a few years before they would have to cede control of India to its people.

The history books look upon almost every action taken by the most prominent pre-Independence freedom fighters as exemplary and skim over the effects of their decisions, including withdrawing the INC from the (limited) governance of several British Indian provinces in 1939, which had been secured through the ballot box. Those who had voted the party into power in any of these locations were seemingly not consulted when this decision was made.[2]

A serial lowering of expectations of the geographic reach of India was evident in the events just before Independence. The INC leadership had repeatedly said that it would never consent to the division of India on the basis of faith, and yet, this is what happened. If Abraham Lincoln had not opposed those who demanded that the Civil War end with the secession of the Confederacy, what would be the position of the US in the international order today? If Mao had remained content with the territorial extent of China during past dynasties and had not added Manchuria, Inner Mongolia, Xinjiang and Tibet to the PRC, what would be the relative position of the PRC in the comity of nations today?

Politicians frequently use the word 'sacrifice', though they have often refused to sacrifice their own interests. They habitually remain more than willing to sacrifice the interests of the people they claim to champion if it serves their own purposes. Ancient India talked not of sacrifice but of wealth and abundance, unlike the lifestyle of the saintly Mahatma Gandhi, who propagated the idea of being content with mere subsistence. Other potential superpowers heard their leaders' calls for efforts to secure prosperity. 'To get rich is glorious', was Deng's mantra.[3] In contrast, Mahatma Gandhi sought to mainstream his own abstemious life. It was, therefore, not a surprise that the same lifestyle continued to be made available to the people of India by the post-1947 leaders who took charge of the destiny of the republic.

STRATEGY: NOT STRUNG FROM BEADS OF TACTICS

The closer an individual is to subsistence, the greater their propensity to look at events and actions from a short-term perspective. There is a difference between 'tactics' (i.e., responses to immediate situations) and 'strategy' (i.e., a plan of action to take advantage of the synergies available in the human and material resources of a country so as to ensure stable progress). In India, policy has usually involved compounding a succession of tactical moves. Every once in a while, the tactics of the immediate past would get bundled together and advertised as the strategy of the leader of the day. There have, of course, been some changes in strategy, for example, having the public sector dominate the economy. It must be said that the later absence of strategy in the portals of government did not exist during the Nehru years. In economic policy, control by the State was considered essential, and encouraging private enterprises to grow was seen as a threat to centralized planning. In foreign policy, Nehru was anchored to the oppressive colonial past, which affected his world view and consequently, his foreign policy in a manner that caused a substantial distance between the US (which was seen as siding with former colonial powers against erstwhile colonies) and India. After Nehru passed away in 1964, the brief period when Lal Bahadur Shastri was the PM saw efforts towards creating an equitable balance in the relations between India and the West, along with moves towards deregulation in economic policy. Unfortunately, the Shastri period was all too brief.

While Shastri did have a strategy similar to Deng's in the PRC nearly two decades later, his successor Indira Gandhi lived from crisis to crisis, always seeking control, fashioning responses as she went along. Once Indira Gandhi took charge as the PM, there was a period of confusion with respect to foreign policy. There were backstage efforts at reconciling with the US while doubling down on the partnership with the USSR. This was a development caused, in large part, by US President Richard Nixon's antipathy towards India and affinity towards the generals in Pakistan, who had served as messengers between the two sides in his reconciliation process with the PRC during the 1970s. Earlier, Poland had been designated for this role, but the problem there was that Warsaw was unable to free itself from the overall Soviet interest of ensuring that the PRC and the US did not come together against the USSR, which is what happened when Pakistan became the go-between. PM Rajiv Gandhi was more overt in reaching out to the US in particular. However, Washington was unwilling to reciprocate in a manner that would have facilitated the rise of India in the same way as it was helping in the rise of China. Rajiv Gandhi did not—or could not—take the leap of downsizing relations with Moscow, and once Mikhail Gorbachev became the general secretary of the Communist Party of the USSR (CPSU) in 1985, there was no longer any need to wean India away from a USSR that, under its new leader, was both complacent and compliant as far as US demands were concerned.

P.V. Narasimha Rao had a strategy similar to Shastri's—the other non-Nehru-Gandhi INC PM of the twentieth century. Having had a longer tenure in office, Shastri's reforms were more in number. Among his key contributions was the initiation of the Green Revolution, which has had enduring benefits. Atal Bihari Vajpayee of the Bharatiya Janata Party (BJP) sought to balance the legacy of the Nehru-Gandhi dynasty with the very instincts for change that were passed on to his government from the base of his party. Despite being tentative, Vajpayee's moves were beneficial. The annual rate of growth increased, together with a loosening of regulations, such as the replacement of the draconian Foreign Exchange Regulation Act (FERA), 1973 with the Foreign Exchange Management Act (FEMA), 1999.

The problem is that strategy is not a necklace strung from the beads of tactics but an entirely different construct that often needs to have a relation to goals outside the tactics of the day, month or even year. The more frequently desirable strategies get executed, the greater the constant alterations in the subsequent mix of tactics to defend against immediate threats and take advantage of present opportunities. The more such changes and adjustments, the greater the congruence between the tactics followed and the strategic framework within which they are implemented. Of course, this assumes the existence of a clear-cut matrix working towards substantive deliverables to improve the lives of the people. What happens in a governance system where the very notion of strategy—other than the woolliest of concepts and philosophies—is dismissed as fanciful, and the focus remains on immediate problem solving and the gratification of the needs of the governance mechanism? Such a path ensures that success within the broader community never becomes mainstream.

A DIVIDED INDIA IS A WEAKER INDIA

The final nail in the colonial coffin designed to straitjacket the Government of India post-Independence was the creation of Pakistan on the irrational grounds that Hindus and Muslims are entirely different people, and that the two religions needed two separate nations. At its core, this propensity for weakening the extent and influence of any succeeding government was based on the belief that the INC would be nowhere near as loyal to British interests as Mohammed Ali Jinnah announced his Muslim League would be once it got the separate country that it was demanding. This idea of the INC's unreliability as a future ally, or even as a closet backer of the Axis, grew on the British officials in Whitehall after Mahatma Gandhi launched the Quit India movement in 1942—the year when it seemed as though the Japanese would overrun India, much as they had other European colonies to the east of the country. In contrast, Jinnah declared his passionate loyalty to the British cause.[4]

In hindsight, were the INC's policy of neutrality during World War II or its decision to dissolve its ministries in 1939 the best courses to follow? Such decisions immeasurably strengthened Jinnah—the self-proclaimed ally of the British against the Axis powers—and his movement for the vivisection of India.

At present, there is little point in cogitating on what may have happened had the stalwarts of the freedom movement held out for a united subcontinent rather than acquiescing to the vivisection of India. They did not. Nor would it be much use to go into what the situation would have been had opportunities been taken advantage of rather than spurned, such as the attempt of the Khan of Kalat or the Ranas of Nepal to accede to India; or if the US and the USSR's informal offer of a permanent seat on the UNSC had been pursued to a successful conclusion; or if the Indian Army had not been prevented by the civilian leadership of the time from taking over the entirety of Jammu and Kashmir rather than remaining content with a truncated state.

Such opportunities were not seized, and the consequences soon became obvious. The Partition was meant to prevent mass killing. Instead, it caused the deaths of more than a million (three million, if subsequent killings of minorities in East and

West Pakistan had been recorded) and the displacement of 15 million,[5] besides widening existing faultlines that are yet to heal. A united India would have had more than 500 million Muslims by now, almost half the Muslim population of the world.[6] This needs to be considered when replying to the question of what, if any, were the gains to the Muslim community in the subcontinent from a partition caused by fanning fears of 'Muslims in danger' and even 'Islam in danger' because of there being more Hindus than Muslims in the subcontinent. Even into the twenty-first century, the same cry echoes across many parts of India by a section of the commentariat, as though a community that numbers close to 200 million[7] can find itself in danger of survival. The biggest losers from Partition have been the Muslims of the subcontinent, who are now divided into three countries, with one having entered the stage of gradual meltdown as a consequence of ethnic and other injustices perpetrated on the population by the force in control of the levers of authority within the state—the military.

It was convenient for a British colonial administration, which presumed the inadequacy of Indians to ever govern themselves, that the INC surrendered the ministries it controlled in 1939. This further advantaged both the colonial administration as well as the Muslim League by ensuring in 1942 that the INC leadership was incarcerated during World War II and left the field of political protest to Jinnah. Furthermore, the British benefitted from the fact that Nehru did not take advantage of the loopholes in the British law and procedure during the 1950s to ensure that more citizens of the Republic of India could migrate to the UK. Passports remained a difficult ask in India until well into the 1980s. During the 1950s, when Pakistan was funnelling hundreds of thousands of its citizens into the UK, those on the other side of the border were denied entry because of the difficulty in getting the papers needed for the journey.[8] Many of the people of Indian descent who settled in Britain went there from places like Uganda, Kenya and Hong Kong rather than from India. The emphasis, as in the past, was on getting everything done through bureaucratic processes, a tendency that persists to this day. For example, conferences and seminars (including those online) involving foreign guests require permission from the Ministry of External Affairs (MEA) and even the Ministry of Home Affairs (MHA). The consequence has been that several conferences organized by Indian entities are held in locations such as Colombo and Kathmandu, often through local platforms, to overcome the delays involved in getting visas for the participants or the permissions to hold the conference in India.

IN PURSUIT OF WHAT SHOULD BE

India's foreign policy after Independence was scripted by Nehru, who had expansive views not on what was realistically possible but on what should be achieved ideally—not only in India but also across the planet. Nehru's breadth of interests is evident in his writings, which have a normative strain. Clearly, he believed that an India led by him had the geopolitical heft needed to nudge the world, especially the Great Powers, onto paths that he favoured. When policy reflects less of 'what is' and more of 'what should be', such actions may end up doing very little to further actual national interest.

At the same time, given the limitations of a recently vivisected India, the impact of our foreign policy on other countries was limited. The eloquence of V.K. Krishna Menon in the United Nations General Assembly (UNGA) failed to move the dial set by geopolitical imperatives. The US and the UK (which was still a great power at that time) had reached the conclusion that India under Nehru was an unreliable partner in Cold War 1.0, which pitted the US and its allies against the USSR and its allies. Given India's foreign and security policies, the US and its allies were not interested in the truth and the just Indian claim over the entirety of Jammu and Kashmir. Instead, they sought to protect the interests of Pakistan against India. Since the 1930s, the Muslim League under Jinnah had battled not against the British but *with* the colonial power *against* the INC—Pakistan was its reward.

Among the axioms taken as gospel by practitioners and theorists of geopolitics and international relations in India, as elsewhere, has been the assessment that 'an unstable Pakistan is not in anyone's interest'. The reality is that a stable Pakistan that remains in the grip of its military is not in the interests of any country, including Pakistan itself. There have been instances in history when foreign and domestic policy have been bent to serve the objectives of those in command of the armed forces, and these have not ended well, as the examples of Japan and Germany in the period preceding and during World War II show. There is a difference between scholarly reflections meant for an entirely academic exercise and policy designed for the real world. The first could safely be based on postulates that represent imagined views of what should be, whereas the latter needs to be anchored in reality.

What could be or should be is different from what is. Policy needs to be scripted on the basis of the latter because designing policy measures based on an imagined construct could prove self-defeating. Take, for instance, the manner in which Tibet's importance to India's water security was ignored while the region was taken over and dominated by the People's Liberation Army (PLA) in the 1950s. In an earlier instance, another oversight was the significance of what is now Pakistan Occupied Kashmir (PoK) to the geopolitical reach of India into Afghanistan and Central Asia, besides increasing India's leverage over a hostile Pakistan and an unpredictable China. The 1947–48 war against tribal invaders sent from Pakistan into Kashmir was halted before the control of the entire territory was returned to New Delhi. Soon afterwards, the PRC was permitted to take control of Aksai Chin, with the Indian side only protesting much later. Furthermore, those in the Intelligence Bureau (IB), or other agencies, who were responsible for this negligence did not face any professional consequences for their actions.

India has a long (and thus far unbroken) tradition of the captains of the bureaucracy ensuring a lack of accountability for the errors of their predecessors. This has led to a lack of attention towards momentous events and the methods used to overcome setbacks. In 2019, in the case of the terror attacks at Uri and Pulwama, there were gaps in the enforcement of security measures. Of course, PM Narendra Modi ensured that the perpetrators of the two attacks paid a heavy price in India or across the border in Pakistan. This has been brought to public attention by the movies made about the exploits of those valorous individuals who took action to avenge these attacks. Given the veil of secrecy that still surrounds so much of the operation of the government, we do not know how those responsible for the initial negligence were identified and punished. They must have been punished. Unlike the way those in the security and military establishment responsible for creating the conditions that resulted in the occupation of posts in Kargil in 1998–99 escaped punishment, with only a lone brigadier serving as the scapegoat for the lapses of those much higher in the ranks. Barring the single scapegoat, the senior officers in the military and intelligence services responsible for the lapses in security caused by the winter withdrawal from border bases that led to Pakistan's Kargil operation were almost all awarded several subsequent promotions. Under PM Modi, accountability has become much more visible. Whether at Uri or Pulwama, or even earlier at Kargil, it must be said that perception management through the media avoided a discussion of the lapses that led to remedial actions against those who were at fault. However, while such measures can, and often do, influence electoral outcomes, the actual situation does not change. Publicity as a substitute for curative activity ensures that problems persist and usually multiply. It is only a matter of time before increasingly higher doses of perception management fail to hold back public response to the reality.

CONSEQUENCES OF CURTAILING PRIVATE INDUSTRY

During World War II, the British government was forced to permit Indian business houses to expand production to help fulfil wartime needs. By 1947, wartime exigencies had made the private sector in India a substantial force, although much smaller in size than what it would have been if the restrictive policies of British rule had not been imposed on Indian businesses, even during wartime, by British PM Winston Churchill. These restrictions had been designed to shield units based in the UK or their subsidiaries from Indian-owned businesses and encourage imports from Britain. During the war, such restrictions on Indian industry had to be loosened by the colonial authorities, given the difficulties in transportation of goods in wartime. As a consequence, private industry in India emerged as a significant force by 1945. This was in contrast to countries that later become economic powerhouses.

For example, war had rendered Japan a devastated country, while the Korean peninsula was unimpressive as an economic force, as indeed were Singapore or Hong Kong. Much of the Middle East had strong linkages with India for centuries, including the widespread use of the Indian rupee, and the same was the case with Southeast Asia. Such bonds began to fray during the 1940s, and never recovered to the earlier levels, when India was the pivot of countries to its west and southeast.

Rather than building on the existing foundations of industry, including the private sector, Nehru, in the early 1950s, decided to adopt a hybrid Soviet system for industries. This was a centralized model based on the assumption that wisdom flowed from the top of the policy chain, and hence, the core decisions for development needed to come from the same source. Nehru also believed that a statist Soviet model was best suited to India, and as a consequence, curbs began to be placed on the private sector to enable the public sector to secure the 'commanding heights' of the economy.

In the case of agriculture, the Zamindari Abolition Act was implemented in 1950, and often involved summary expropriation. The takeover of land sans compensation paved the road for future takeovers by private industry. This had consequences for the relative position of India vis-à-vis some other Asian countries that were more permissive of private initiative and enterprise. A country makes progress when its more advanced elements have the freedom to develop their capacities without being slowed down, or worse, blocked entirely by the governance mechanism. While several of the zamindars were neglectful of their lands, some of those who succeeded them were clueless about how to raise output per acre. After declining yields and famines, it was only towards the close of the 1960s that the Green Revolution (assisted by US experts) supervised by a business-friendly minister (C. Subramaniam) succeeded in putting India onto the path of agricultural self-sufficiency.

Had the private sector and entrepreneurship in India been encouraged in the manner that South Korea and Japan began doing during the 1950s, the Indian economy and external trade would have grown far more than the unimpressive rates of growth that characterized the era of Nehru and Indira Gandhi. Only in 1992 were several of the restrictions on private industry removed by the central government. The loss of growth by then was substantial.

When India secured its freedom, the private sector was potentially capable of propelling the country forward at rates of growth far higher than what was seen during the 1950s and the 1960s. Instead of creating an environment for businesses to grow, several lines of production as well as the power to make even routine decisions were denied to them, on the grounds that the 'commanding heights' of the economy needed to be located within the public sector. A country's industrial structure—like a pyramid—necessitates a healthy micro, small and medium enterprises (MSME) sector to sustain large industries. And while it may be possible to closely monitor and even superintend a few large enterprises, hundreds of thousands of smaller enterprises are difficult to direct. The command economy, with its licencing and regulatory requirements, created a situation where enterprises that could persuade decision-makers at the concerned levels to go along with their plans grew in number, while genuine innovators lacking such skills faltered and were often forced to shut shop. Those with an in with policymakers used their skills less to improve their products and more to ensure that their potential rivals were prevented from entering the market. Such games are played to this day. The armoury of weapons available to derail an enterprise has remained sizeable over time, ranging from misuse of the leeway given by the justice system, to the reality of any of the multiple layers of decision-making being able to stop, or at the least substantially delay, an enterprise from going into production mode. Increasingly, such methods are being used by foreign suppliers and their agents in India to stop local competition from developing, even in fields where the latter have had a track record of low costs and high-quality outputs. The use of false cases to kneecap innovators that threaten foreign imports has long been a reality in India, although the situation has changed significantly, especially during the second term of PM Modi, which began in 2019. Many have asked why Indians do so well in countries such as the US or the UK while being unable to replicate similar success at home. The answer may be found in the colonial model of government, which still remains embedded in many of our governmental procedures. Leaders like P.V. Narasimha Rao or Modi have sought to create a policy ecosystem that facilitates innovation and enterprise rather than choke it. Much has been accomplished, especially during Modi 2.0, but this is still a work in progress.

Government intervention has had a chilling effect on the success of genuine entrepreneurs (those who rely not on contacts but on innovation and enterprise). Since the 1980s, the information technology (IT) industry in India had a track record of extraordinary rates of growth, until the Vajpayee government introduced the Information Technology Act in 2000. HCL, Wipro, Infosys and many other IT stars all began before such laws and attendant regulations were introduced. For several years after the IT Act became law, there was a lack of another domestic champion of their size springing up. Thus, one may conclude that the IT industry in India was flourishing while it was outside the regulatory net of the IT Act, 2000.

In democracies that favour innovation, citizens are given the freedom to innovate, except in those fields that are explicitly banned. In a colonial culture, the reverse is true. The citizens are barred from doing anything other than what the government permits them to do. It is, therefore, no surprise that so many find success not within the country but by moving to another. The governance system fails to understand that the everyday citizen of India, especially in the twenty-first century, performs best when left alone rather than when they have to constantly seek official approval. If more cases of the delays and failures caused by such policies were brought before the public in a manner far more prominent than what has been the case thus far, the popular opinion could have mobilized to make the slogan of 'Minimum government, maximum governance' a reality. Despite measures such as the Right to Information, the level of transparency and accountability within the administration in India is inadequate. This is why almost every officer of some of the central services reaches higher pay scales before retiring with a comfortable pension.

RECLAIMING A BYGONE POTENCY

A retrospective look provides useful insights into India's declining footprint from 1932 to the Sino-Indian border conflict in 1962. In 1932, 15 years before Independence, New Delhi was the centre of decision-making for a large territory. Imagine an eagle with its wings sweeping into Southeast Asia and the Middle East, and its head entering Tibet, with talons deep inside the western segment of the Indo-Pacific. India's currency was the most convenient medium of exchange, and its views were taken on board when policy was being formulated within this expansive stretch of land and sea. In 1962, 15 years after Independence, India stood alone when it was savaged by the PLA, a crisis caused by poor leadership—both civilian and military—that led to a fall in Indian prestige and influence even greater than what had followed the partition of the subcontinent and the earlier breaking away of the constituents of South Asia.[9]

The reality is that the New Delhi of 1962 was a much-diminished version of the capital in 1932. Understanding this reality and drawing lessons from it is central to the design and implementation of any strategy formulated to ensure that the eagle of the geopolitical heft of India reclaims its earlier potency and indeed, increases the wingspan of its influence.

Opportunities may get created or they may exist, awaiting utilization. A factual rendering of the history of the subcontinent in various periods has yet to be made. For a long time, when India was in the control of alien entities, it was to be expected that the only opportunities seized by the ruling powers would be those that benefitted not this country but the alien rulers and their interests. Once the country gained Independence, one could reasonably have expected the governments taking charge of the administration to be on the lookout for any opportunity to improve the nation's situation. The history taught in schools and universities concentrates on discovering the positive, such as the fact that the abysmal condition in which the British left India was improved. That was certainly the case, but when the context is restricted to India, it goes unmentioned that several other countries in Asia did much better on numerous parameters of human needs, despite having gone through very destructive periods.[10] Lee Kuan Yew, the founding father of the independent city state of Singapore, is said to have quipped, perhaps not in jest, that he had studied the experience of India, especially its policies and progress, so as to know which paths to avoid in his efforts to modernize Singapore.[11]

The many missteps of the Nehruvian foreign policy, discussed earlier in this chapter, are covered only in passing, if at all, in school and college curricula, even though this series of missed or botched opportunities has made the whole of India less than what ought to be the sum of its parts. Elementary, middle and high-school education needed to get pride of place, while the restrictions that were placed on starting private institutions were avoidable. One of the most valuable possessions that the departing British left India were not the buildings in the Lutyens Zone but the English language, which was downgraded as a matter of state policy. Knowledge of English—the international link language—would have been an invaluable aid in expanding opportunities for learning and work, yet this was neglected in State-run schools. As a consequence, those too poor to afford private education or get tuitions in the English language later lost out to others who could afford to attend private schools. It was only during 1984–89, under PM Rajiv Gandhi, that greater attention began to be paid to enable students in government-run schools to get a working knowledge of English.

Despite this, the learning of English remained out of reach of the underprivileged and was monopolized by those at the higher levels of the income chain. Many of the seats in quality institutions were occupied by students from relatively better-off sections of society. In an ironic example of how higher education subsidized for the benefit of the poor very often ended up benefitting those who were better off, it was said of the Medical College Thiruvananthapuram that the fees paid to learn medicine in that institution could not even cover the cost of the plaster on the walls of its buildings. Expectedly, considering the skewness in the education system, very few of the genuinely underprivileged secured admission to the college. To this day, admission to the higher class of government-run institutions is mostly obtained by those with sufficient funds and a supportive ecosystem suited to passing the entrance examinations for these institutions.

A WEALTH IN PEOPLE, A TRAGEDY IN POLICY

The wealth of India is its people. The tragedy of India is the matrix of policies that has prevented its people from taking advantage of the opportunities available across different periods of time. The governance system has long been obsessed with process rather than product. As long as processes (that are usually far more cumbersome than desirable) are followed, the product or the lack thereof has seldom been a hindrance to an official career.

British officials acted within the decision-making matrix as though the people of India were children in need of round-the-clock adult supervision. The perception was that the government knows what is best for the ordinary citizen, better than them, and this has refused to fade away. Given the overall intellectual fit between present and pre-1947 methods of selection and training, it should not be a surprise that the mindset of the higher echelons of the Indian civil service—comprising the Indian Administrative Services (IAS), Indian Foreign Services (IFS) and Indian Police Services (IPS), and the middle echelons of the Railway, Forest, Revenue and other services—sometimes seem, in practice, to be tethered to the same view of Indian people's capabilities for independent thought and action (or belief in the lack thereof).

In Afghanistan, the road from Kabul to Kandahar has roadblocks at different spots, where a tithe must be paid to get through. The system of decision-making in India, at almost every level, follows much the same model. Successive levels of decision-makers have to be persuaded to approve the necessary permissions. Tracking a file for a particular project—such as the setting up of a large industrial unit—reveals the multiplicity of layers involved in the decision-making process, with files often moving up and down or remaining static at select levels without much apparent effort to ensure a faster disposal of the matter. This is particularly true of those projects where special interest is not shown by the concerned authority.

Public administration needs an ambience of genuine pride within the policymaking community of the country and confidence in its future. If neither are present, the administration is likely to skim off as much as possible from individual cases and squirrel away these resources, including on foreign shores. Since the 1990s, in a trend that had been increasingly visible during the 1980s, much, if not all, the tithes, collected as a consequence of affixing a signature on a decision, have been deposited outside the country, usually to locations where close family members of the administrators are sent to settle down and establish themselves, awaiting the arrival of the benefactor after they complete their service back home. Whether it is Singapore, Toronto, New York, London or other cities with globalized banking systems, there are growing clusters of former Indian nationals who receive large amounts of money from exotic locales as recompense for their 'work'—the nature and extent of which is neither obvious nor apparent. The common factor in such transactions is that these fortunate citizens have a familial or other such connection with individuals in India who are part of, or close to, the governance structure, and who ensure a steady flow of money into the pockets of their foreign nominees. When in the recesses of the mind of an official, the country is regarded as less than first-rate and its people are seen as needing supervision rather than autonomy of activity, settling for second- or third-rate outcomes at a price, rather than holding out for the best, becomes standard practice.

The IFS has some outstanding officers, as do the IAS, the IPS and others. However, regulations and excessive procedures designed to block a single weed often come at the cost of several hundreds of healthy plants being sacrificed. For instance, the immense soft power of the Indian diaspora often gets underutilized, unlike other countries (including Pakistan) that trawl such shoals with much greater rigour and effect. In several countries across the globe, there are members of the Indian diaspora that have immense personal and, in some cases, business influence over top officials. Such individuals need to be systematically identified so that persons of influence have access to not just envoys but, in some cases, to the top rungs of the Government of India. Should there be an effort on the part of official institutions to locate such individuals and seek to persuade them to be helpful in ways that promote better relations between India and their countries of residence, there would be much more value than in the endless courtesy calls and photo opportunities of Indian dignitaries with their counterparts abroad. It is only after Modi took over as the PM in 2014 that the diaspora has become a primary focus of attention for both the MEA as well as the Prime Minister's Office (PMO).

It must be said that our diplomats abroad work very hard to establish relationships, only to lose contact once their brief tenures in the concerned capital end. Some return after a few years to relationships that are different in quality from what they had left behind. It is not accidental that the USSR and the PRC, for example, began to keep envoys in one place for long periods of time, once it became apparent that the relationships that were cultivated by the diplomat in question were too valuable to risk losing. Envoys from these countries (as also later Russia) typically stayed in their posts for long periods of time, enough to develop substantial networks of friendship and influence. In contrast, Indian envoys were routinely rotated out after a few years to make way for other officers. The new envoys often had to build up personal ties with key officials from the start, given that such relationships are not a wristwatch that can be passed on from one individual to the other. However, in the Indian system, rotation is given priority over such considerations.

In a complex economy and evolving society such as India, the governance mechanism should attempt to substitute the headwind created by slow growth across sectors and populations with the tailwind of fast growth as much as possible. After 15 August 1947, the steel frame of the colonial-era civil service lovingly tended to and put in place by our leaders has sought to control civil society rather than act as an enabler of its progress through policy-induced changes in the external environment, and in the pathways towards expanding the capacities of as many citizens as possible. The objective of a system geared to control and not achieve becomes procedures and not outcomes, which is made easier by a lack of accountability. Greater control has been preferred over greater expansion, lest the latter necessitate reduced supervision of the administrative mechanism over the other elements of society, including industry and civil society, which have been subjected to a much smaller dose of individual freedom in India than has been the case in the US, for example. The consequence was a 'less productive' Indian, who moved to the US and increased his productivity manifold in that more permissive environment.

2

The Rise of China and Cold War 2.0

Just as the US and the USSR were, in a previous era, locked in Cold War 1.0, the PRC and the US are now engaged in Cold War 2.0. The first Cold War was existential and ended only with the dissolution of the USSR in 1991. It was a battle, not just between two nations, but also between two competing and contradictory systems of governance. For a considerable period of time, the USSR seemed to be gaining on the US. Countries around the world were introducing elements of the Soviet system into their own systems of governance. An early example, dating back to the 1950s, was India. Central planning was introduced to the joy of the bureaucracy, and until 1967, the INC, almost without exception, ruled comfortably in the states as well as the Centre.

India claimed to be non-aligned but leant towards Russia, partly owing to the errors of the Indian leadership as well as those of Washington, which, for three decades after World War II ended, took its cues about South America, Africa and Asia from European powers that wished to retain their colonial-era influence over the three continents. This weakened much of the soft power appeal of the US in countries that watched the superpower routinely adopt European priorities and attitudes in interactions with them. In contrast, the USSR proclaimed an 'anti-colonial' crusade, even as the Kremlin made certain that its Eastern European satellites had very little autonomy in practice. What happened in Hungary and Czechoslovakia (now the Czech Republic and Slovakia), and partly in Poland, was visibly the Soviet version of the colonialization of South America, Asia and Africa by the UK, France, Spain, Belgium and the Netherlands. The only difference was that the level of brutality committed by the latter against the indigenous people of the colonized continents was incomparably higher.

NAVIGATING COLD WAR 2.0

In the era of Cold War 2.0, across the years, elements of the governance system practised in the PRC have been resonating with parts of the world that are considered democratic. Whether it is in Poland or Hungary and, to an extent, even in Denmark, elements resembling autocracy have made a comeback. Since 2020, with the onset of the Covid-19 pandemic, government power has substantially expanded into everyday lives, and the rollback of such expansion may be slow, even after the pandemic subsides. The rate of growth of the PRC has not just been admired but efforts have also been made to emulate it, just as the USSR was emulated in its days of sputniks and space travel. Despite its authoritarian structure, the PRC has been moving ahead in the knowledge economy and has used diplomacy as well as trade and other instruments to ensure that any response to its progress towards primacy remains scattered and uncoordinated. Even in the US, what is considered to be the Right has made a comeback and joined the Left, seeking strong leadership, of course, in their own separate way. The continuing influence of the 'Strongman' President Donald Trump in nearly 40 per cent of the US electorate reflects an ancient hunger for strong leadership in a situation of confusion and seeming chaos. The signs are becoming obvious that the battle of systems and for primacy between the US and the PRC is as existential as the one between the US and USSR had been.

Until recently, all that needed to be done to ensure kinetic intervention by the US, its European allies, or both, in Asian, African and South American countries was for anti-regime elements in these countries to persuade their major partners in the NATO that a takeover by elements considered hostile to its interests was imminent unless military force was used. Of course, it needs to be added that there were examples of attempted takeovers of state structures by communists, say, in Chile or Vietnam, with great success. However, these were the exceptions. Usually, it was those who had lost their privileges to a new group of rulers who cried 'communist'. Take, for instance, former PM Mohammad Mosaddeq of Iran, who came from an aristocratic background and, yet was labelled a communist and overthrown in a coup orchestrated by the Central Intelligence Agency (CIA).

Yet, despite such exertions, more and more countries slipped into the Soviet orbit, while Ho Chi Minh received enough assistance (mainly from Moscow and somewhat less from Beijing) to defeat the US and unify Vietnam by the mid-1970s. The spectacle of defeat at the hands of a 'peasant' army further damaged the US' efforts to roll back the pro-Soviet tide. Cold War 1.0 got its impetus from the Korean War, which ended in a stalemate that continues to smoulder. Going by the public opinion outside much of China, the origins and spread of Covid-19 in 2020 provided the breakout moment for Cold War 2.0.

That a new Cold War has begun, which is also existential and will end in the collapse of either the American or Chinese system of governance, was disputed, indeed derided, by several analysts.[1] Varying arguments have been used to support their scepticism. Some say that the volume of trade between the PRC and the US is so huge that it effectively precludes anything more deadly than a form of shadow boxing, where blows are seemingly landed but, in reality, they are not. They contrast this with the trade relations between the USSR and the US, which were much smaller, as were the accompanying linkages between the two. Others scoff at the characterization of the CCP as communist at all, pointing to the substantial number of high-net-worth individuals in the Party, especially so in the higher echelons.[2] They take heart from examples such as Jiang Zemin's admission of inducting not just 'capitalist roaders'[3] but capitalists themselves into the CCP, something that would have been anathema to Mao.[4] Fortunately for Jiang, this innovation that he introduced occurred much later in his decade of rule (1993–2003); else, he would not have escaped the punishment for apostasy that was meted out by Mao to many party members during his lifetime.

Another way to deny the reality of Cold War 2.0 is to claim that it will resemble Cold War 1.0 in its overall characteristics, which, of course, is an absurd way of looking at the development. Even at the end of the 1930s, some generals (many in the French army of the time) believed that the next war with Germany would follow the same pattern as what had taken place during World War I. Similarly, there are those who believe that if there is a cold war between the US and the PRC, the way there was one between the USSR and the US, it would need to follow the same pattern, and hence, is not simply improbable but impossible. Unfortunately for them, the transparency introduced in the CCP leadership's goals by General Secretary Xi Jinping has made the reality of

Cold War 2.0 difficult to deny or otherwise overlook.

The fact is that long before the advent of Xi to the top, the CCP leadership core was aware that they were engaged in a battle of systems with the US, and that this would end in the defeat of one or the other of the two superpowers. Considerable attention has been focussed by the security services of the PRC towards monitoring groups and individuals who are pro-West—specifically, pro-US. Large pools of the population, such as the Christian community, are being watched because they are considered more susceptible to influences that believe the communist system (including the one followed by the PRC) to be inherently evil and needs replacement.

Deng Xiaoping, however, was no capitalist roader at heart (as he was alleged to be by some of followers of Mao, including his spouse), but the opposite.[5] Deng believed in the 'communist system with Chinese characteristics,'[6] and the party overshadowed all else for him. It was to strengthen the CCP that Deng pushed for the economic reforms that were introduced in the 1980s. Deng understood that a shaky economy would not maintain its grip over the state power of the CCP for long, and therefore, it was an existential necessity to speed up economic growth. It was a surprise to many PRC watchers in the Atlanticist world that Deng paid very little attention to political reform, even as he pushed ahead with revolutionary innovations in economic policy. The grip of the CCP over the individual remained as intact as it had been during Mao's years in power. Viewed in this light, his decision to send tanks into Tiananmen Square in 1989 ought to have been forecast much before the protest built up to a level that, according to the CCP leadership core, crossed into active subversion of the monopoly of the CCP's rule.

Deng expected General Secretary Zhao Ziyang to wield the

iron fist through a velvet glove. During the Tiananmen Square developments, Zhao's soft side (which was the misleading face of the PRC leadership that Deng wanted the US, in particular, to see)[7] was revealed to not just be a mask but a dominant part of his personality. So, Deng instantly replaced him with a hardliner. The difference in treatment meted out to billionaires by Xi and Jiang ought to have been predicted when the public comments by the former in 2013 clarified that he was steeped in Mao Zedong Thought in a manner that Jiang obviously never was. In his responses to those seen as less than kosher, Xi resembles Mao much more than he ever resembled Deng, the second of the three foundational leaders of the PRC—Mao, Deng and Xi.

CHINA: A DRIVE FOR GLOBAL PRIMACY

Given that Xi resembles Mao, it ought not to have been a surprise when Xi began rolling out a series of initiatives from 2013 onwards that were visibly designed to catapult China above the US in the global primacy sweepstakes. The fanfare in the rollout of the Belt and Road Initiative (BRI), initially known as the One Belt One Road (OBOR) initiative, was impossible to miss. Xi has long cogitated to ensure that most of the countries in Europe replace the US with the PRC in their logistical chains and create a network of routes and facilities that would be difficult to not be a part of. China's BRI links the whole of Eurasia together in a manner not seen before in history and is in line with Mao's vision of the PRC recovering its status as the Middle Kingdom of the world from the US—the latest western usurper to seek that title. There was much less ostentation behind the effort by Xi to ensure that when the US dollar (USD) suffered a reset, the renminbi (RMB) would be ready at the top of the basket of alternatives to replace it as the reserve currency of the globe. This was a force multiplier that Xi wanted to see eliminated from Washington's arsenal. Xi has pursued this objective through quiet moves towards an almost cashless society in many Chinese cities. These moves occurred at accelerating speed during his period in office as a consequence of public acceptance over time (in contrast to the shock of demonetization in India undertaken at PM Modi's fiat in 2016). More and more citizens of the PRC are using their mobile phones in financial transactions, rather than using paper currency. The outlines of Xi's plan to benefit from the dollar reset, which he is working towards with President Vladimir Putin in Moscow, are apparent in PRC's initiatives of turning to blockchain as a means of gaining international confidence in the transparency of the planned Chinese digital currency, and replacing the USD with the RMB in transactions with a growing list of countries.[8]

Another strand is in the planning designed to counter the US military superiority. This objective predates Xi, for it had been initiated by his predecessor Hu Jintao (2002–12) during his period in office. Xi has expanded Hu's initial moves and public calls for the PLA to become a force that can overawe and, where necessary, defeat the US. Military bases are being created in the PRC, both openly and in the guise of civilian projects. The PLA has multiplied its weapons systems by adding those with advanced technology. By the 2030s, there are likely to be a total of at least six aircraft carriers in the PLA Navy (PLAN), boosting its capacity for force projection in theatres of war it previously could not reach.[9] The PLA Air Force (PLAAF) has also been strengthened, with substantial help from Moscow. Outlets that reflect the views of the leadership core are no longer wary of referring to the PRC replacing the US as the primary power on the globe and even in claiming that a military victory over China is no longer possible for the US and its partners within the Indo-Pacific.[10] Having created independent linkages with the EU members, including getting them involved in the BRI, the planners around Xi are concerned with the US rather than with the other members of NATO.[11] The belief in Beijing is that only Washington has the nerve and the firepower to initiate a kinetic situation in certain circumstances. The other members of NATO would never initiate such a conflict, even when the expansion of power by the PRC (mostly in theatres of war located in the Indo-Pacific) continues apace, as Xi intends should happen.[12]

REIMAGINING THE PRC

Cold War 1.0 had multiple 'fronts,' and not just in battlefields. The areas of the conflict included universities and companies, civil society through NGOs and a 'tech war' using the power of several high-tech mechanisms to cause problems to the opposing party. Despite this, there are those who misunderstand the nature of a cold war by looking only at kinetic conflict (involving weapons and militaries) as defining war. Interestingly, the CCP leadership core has been aware for a considerable period that the PRC and the US were in a state of war in a non-kinetic manner. The PRC has been creating networks comprising agents of influence and outright spies within the EU, US and other target countries, including India, at speed at least since the period when Hu was general secretary of the CCP. Simultaneously, the regime in Beijing has been making intense efforts at identifying and neutralizing the US and other target country networks in China. Such neutralization had taken place even during the Jiang tenure, which was relatively the most benign to US interests in the post-Deng period. Jiang was content to expand trade and profits for those involved in trade, and was not as attentive as Hu later was to the fact that much of the technology in the products used by the PRC came from outside the country. It was during his time that fusions were attempted between western and local culture, including music. What emerged from the mix was a confusing cacophony of sound and dance in which raw energy and spectacle sought to compensate for the quality of talent.

Slowly, pride of place began to be given to what was defined within the CCP as 'Chinese' culture, although fusion remained welcome and western strands retained pride of place. All this gave way after Xi took over as general secretary of the CCP in 2012. In a sign of differentiation between Mao Zedong Thought and Xi Jinping Thought, Confucius was readmitted into the pantheon of greats of the past, while the western element in much of programming was downgraded, even as the Chinese element became ascendant. No longer did history begin in 1922, when the CCP was formed, or in 1949, when the PRC came into existence. Since the Hu period, efforts at renovating ancient ruins and other cultural treasures that had long been neglected, if not forgotten, have been intensified. At the heart of CCP General Secretary Xi's appeal to the people of the PRC was the significant manner in which the PLA was placed at the centre of the national renaissance. The need for the Chinese people to once again be at the apex of human endeavour and civilization, which had earlier been invoked almost subliminally, has been taken out of the closet and flashed in technicolour by Xi.[13]

There is more. While Jiang sought to connect with (mainly wealthy) ethnic Han people who had settled abroad, Xi has placed his loyalty in the fulfilment of the China Dream as the civilizational duty of the Han people wherever they may be—in Penang or Vancouver or Edinburgh. Ethnic Han people are, in effect, called upon to ensure that their actions are congruent with the higher loyalty required for the Middle Kingdom (otherwise known as the PRC) to establish its deserved primacy in the superintendence of global affairs.[14] This may, on occasion, involve 'special tasks,' and secondary loyalties (to the country that they are citizens of, for instance) to not be permitted to stand in the way of such a 'historical duty.'

There is a method in the strident militaristic and triumphalist tone being used by Xi and those close to his way of thinking. This campaign has been designed to revitalize Han ethnonationalism, so that they flame up and remove any hesitation within the public to obey the guidelines for each member of the global Han community. These will, of course, be set by the doctrine of a Han-centric drive to re-establish the 'normal' equilibrium of the Middle Kingdom's centrality in a fractious world.

Interestingly, the authoritarian system of governance established by the CCP under Mao that has continued into its present is beginning to be emulated even in Europe—whether in Hungary or even Poland. Among political leaders, the 'nice guy' is being steadily displaced by 'strongmen' even within the EU. In the past, when the competition was with the USSR, a shift of systems involved a visible change in governance models, whereas, during Cold War 2.0, coming closer to the 'China Model' involves more subtle alterations. Authoritarianism comes in slices from the margins, not in chunks that are impossible to miss or to explain away. Blocking one's own head of state, in this case former US President Trump, from an online platform controlled by a private company is now seen as an act of almost liberal excellence—such has been the permeation of the influence of the China Model under Xi.[15] Arbitrary actions have become increasingly common. For instance, in Canada, the bank accounts of those who contributed even $50 to the truckers' strike were frozen.[16] Similarly, the assets of individuals considered close to President Putin, even when their passports are not Russian, were confiscated.[17] Due process is essential to the rule of law, and its dilution of this, no matter what the motive, needs to be seen in this context.

General Secretary Xi, aware that the economic growth of the PRC may not be what it had been in the regimes of his two predecessors, has moved away from reliance merely on their gross domestic product (GDP) and rates of its annual growth to a message stressing the hard power of the military and the strong will of the Chinese (read Han) people to overcome obstacles and re-establish themselves as the core of human achievement and prominence. Cold War 2.0 is on between the US and the PRC, and it is, once again, a battle of systems, with a generous dash of ethnonationalism. The fault lines created by the Cold War 2.0 have opened up an opportunity for India, which has become as essential a partner to the US in the new situation as China was when the USSR had been the adversary. The advent of the new Cold War 2.0 will result in a steady moving away of several manufacturing units from the PRC to other locations, and India could be the principal beneficiary of this. However, unless this opportunity is understood and utilized, in the manner that the PRC did in this decade itself, its potential dividend will go to waste.

INSIDIOUS INFLUENCE: CHINA'S SOFTER APPROACH

Just as the USSR bunched around itself a group of countries that were, in varying degrees, ready to challenge the US primacy and interests on a broad front, so too has the PRC successfully assembled a group of countries that (again to varying degrees) have come together to challenge the US's global primacy and its consequences.[18] Just as several countries that are part of the US-led system are less involved in it because of their affinity for the US but more due to the need and perceived interests of the governments, so is the case with countries that are affiliating with the PRC. Countries that regard it as incompatible to their interests to accept the proportion of Washington's agenda in return for US protection now have an alternative superpower to which they can turn.

In the case of the US, countries need to vocally advertise their fealty or close friendship to the country that has had such a pivotal role in fashioning the post-1945 world. Some may say the PRC is more subtle. The CCP leadership core favours a modern variant of the Jimifuzhou (Jimi) system prevalent in the Tang dynasty, more than a millennium and a half ago. In this system, the emperor and his court accepted the formal protocols designed to give outward honour and respect to a lesser power while making sure that the latter followed policies and acted in a manner designed to promote the objectives of the Middle Kingdom. The external show of respect masked the reality of internal acquiescence to the wishes of the emperor and his court.

A recent example of the PRC's modern-day implementation of the Jimifuzhou is Turkey. Its President Recep Tayyip Erdoğan has signed an extradition agreement with Beijing that will mainly be directed at those in the Uygur community who are within the reach of Turkish authorities.[19] The Uygurs of Xinjiang consider themselves to be of Turkic origin, as do some other nationalities in Central Asia. They have looked upon Ankara as the defendant of what they see as a movement to protect their autonomy and culture from getting overwhelmed by the influence of Han culture and the authority of the Chinese state. Unfortunately for them, their supposed champion has turned towards the PRC. The bonhomie between Beijing and Ankara became visible when Erdoğan assisted Azerbaijan to claw back significant portions of Nagorno-Karabakh from Armenian control.[20] The Armenia-Azerbaijan conflict in 2020 was marked by Moscow's reluctance to intervene on Armenia's side in the decisive manner that was needed to ensure that Azerbaijan not succeed in its conquest for territory. Instead, it was Azerbaijan that received assistance from a military allied to the PLA—Pakistan—besides, of course, Turkey.[21] Sophisticated tactics were used to overcome the Armenian defences, and in all likelihood, Beijing was instrumental in persuading Russia not to intervene until the Azeris were satisfied. China (through the Pakistan Army) guided the Azerbaijan military in the use of drones and other high-performance assets to devastating effect. The military of Russia is highly competent in using drones and other such technologies to ensure victory on the battlefield. These were evidently not shared with Armenia, despite the security pact between Yerevan and Moscow. The Armenian government had been flirting with the US and some of the bigger NATO partners, but expectedly, neither Washington nor Brussels gave any assistance to the orthodox Christian power that was seeking to get closer to them, a factor that may have helped motivate Putin to sit the Armenia-Azerbaijan conflict out on the sidelines, thereby pleasing the General Headquarters (GHQ) of the Pakistan Army in Rawalpindi (the effective centre of power in the country rather than the political establishment in Islamabad) and its 'all weather' force-multiplying 'iron partner'—the PLA.

AN INTERNAL FOCUS

Both Mao and Deng sought to transform the PRC. While Mao assisted attempted insurrections in a limited manner, including in India, he was as clear about the principle of 'Socialism in One Country' being relevant to China as Joseph Stalin was about its validity for the USSR. Unlike Vladimir Lenin and Leon Trotsky, Stalin concentrated entirely on what he saw as the interests of the USSR. Trotsky, in particular, was a forebearer of the dreams of Che Guevara, who tried to replicate the Cuban revolution in other parts of South America and lost his life in the attempt. Trotsky called for 'Permanent Revolution,' and for the USSR to lead the charge designed to get other countries to turn to communism. In contrast, Stalin focussed on his own country far too obsessively, judging by the casualty count of the Red Terror that he presided over, until the German invasion of 1941, when his attention was drawn to that conflict rather than eliminating the many whom he regarded as antithetical to his rule.

Given his dislike for the manner in which Moscow treated Beijing as a junior partner, it was Mao who initiated the move towards befriending the US. This was an objective that was in his mind even during the 1950s, judging by some of his asides to guests.[22] The import of Mao's actions was not read correctly, unlike the ping-pong games that convinced Washington that Beijing was looking for its friendship. Mao's desire to swim in the

Mississippi river[23] was taken as a pleasant aside by Washington, rather than as a hint to the US to cosy up to China. Only after the US table tennis team was invited to Beijing and got a warm reception there was it clear that Mao was interested in mending ties with the US administration, a signal that President Nixon did not fail to pick up. President Nixon sent Henry Kissinger on his epochal mission to Beijing in 1971 to successfully conclude this episode, continue the meltdown of the USSR, and also, for lesser reasons, such as Washington requiring Beijing's help in extricating the US from the quagmire of the Vietnam war with some semblance of its honour intact. Kissinger pushed the Kuomintang (KMT) and Taiwan under the bus in his eagerness to get Mao and Zhou Enlai to agree to a tacit understanding that both would, in multiple ways, seek to destroy the USSR as a political entity. In other exchanges, he encouraged Beijing to start another border war with India, a conflict where the US promised to take the side of the PRC against the world's most populous democracy.[24] Unfortunately for him and for Yahya Khan, Pakistan's dictator at the time of the Bangladesh Liberation War, Mao and Zhou refused the bait. The fear of intervention by the USSR, kindled by the Indo-Soviet Treaty of Peace, Friendship and Cooperation of 1971, played a key role in such forbearance. Similar to Mao, Deng, in his policy changes, focussed on the interests of the PRC as defined by the CCP leadership. As was the case under Mao, the internal changes during Deng's tenure were phenomenal.

The objective of winning back the position of being the Middle Kingdom is being discussed openly in the PRC these days. General Secretary Xi has introduced a degree of transparency about the CCP's objectives that had been absent during Deng's tenure. Under Xi, there have been tides of change in the policy of Beijing towards different countries and the impact these policies have had. An example is the changes triggered by the BRI in individual countries. The BRI marks China's reclamation of its primacy in the Eurasian landmass. The Maritime Silk Road seeks to achieve the same, initially in the Indo-Pacific, but later (together with Moscow) in the Atlantic. From the viewpoint of the international community, the PLA has become a prominent presence, far more so than at any period since the fall from grace of Defence Minister Lin Biao in 1971. PRC diplomacy has been unusually active, and there is little doubt that the agencies of the CCP, other than those dealing with foreign policy, must be similarly activated in an unprecedented manner. The leadership of the CCP has a treasure trove of information about hundreds of thousands of 'people of influence' in countries across the globe. Much of this information has been secured by trawling social media and from the data generated by the multiplicity of mobile applications in which the PRC is becoming the dominant player in the world, displacing the US and leaving the EU and other competitors far behind.[25]

Before a conventional conflict is initiated, it will be possible, using artificial intelligence (AI), to affect and, in some cases, alter the situation on the home front of the country or countries that are on the target list of the PLA. Social fault lines will be mapped and ways found to ensure that social media platforms and particular civil groups get used to expanding the destructive scope of the covert PRC efforts against a target country. The rapid dissemination of hostile messaging, once backed by the ribcage of organization and funding, has the potential to create chaos in the streets. Indeed, this has long been a favoured tactic of the US in countries such as Venezuela and Ukraine. Now, the same methods have been studied and further perfected by the relevant political and government infrastructure in both Moscow as well as China, to be deployed where judged necessary. In Xi, the PRC again has a leader, after Mao, who is willing to take substantial risks in his efforts at securing desirable outcomes. Neither Deng nor Jiang or Hu would have gone down the road that General Secretary Xi is travelling on.

OF NUCLEAR PROXIES AND THE CHINESE THREAT

The contradictions between the US and the PRC have reached a level where many policymakers in Washington have finally accepted that the competition between the two countries is not a friendly contest but is, in its own way, existential.[26] Consequently, the importance of India as a partner has increased exponentially, especially for the US. This has led to the steady deepening of the India–US relations, during the tenures of the US presidents Barack Obama, Trump or now Joe Biden in the White House. India's role as a significant net security provider has increased the investment in the country, so has its access to global markets that had formerly set up blocks against it.[27] Beijing's authoritarian model of governance is gaining support in chancelleries across the world, even as the appeal of the Washington model is fading. Emerging as the biggest economy in the world would be a force multiplier that may make it easier for China to increase the distance in achievement between itself and the US. Similarly, the increasing presence of the 'peace loving,'[28] albeit armed with deadly force, PLA, is allowing regimes, which have long been kept in check over attracting a kinetic reaction from the US, to relook at their acquiescence with the US. Just as the USSR offered an alternative to the US that, at first glance, appeared to have fewer strings attached than moving closer to the US, so is the PRC offering itself as an alternative to the US when the latter is openly hostile, as seen in locations like Venezuela and Iran.

Such flexibility in partnerships applies to countries that are rivals or even overt enemies of countries that Beijing believes are in the US orbit (despite the often-plaintive denials of such a situation by some of the target countries). Although NATO has, from the start, been regarded as a potentially hostile alliance, its members, like France and Germany, have not precluded efforts by the PRC to establish close ties with them. Although India is in a situation where its military is confronting the PLA across the Sino-Indian frontier, Chinese companies have intensified their efforts at grabbing a big a chunk of the Indian market. Even after the kinetic contests of 2017 and 2020 between India and China, the trade surplus of the latter has increased substantially during 2021 and remains on course to repeat its good performance in 2022. The Democratic People's Republic of Korea (DPRK) has long served as an unwelcome distraction for Japan from substantially focussing on the PRC. Indeed, Beijing has been adept at planning to get its future targets to lower their guard and assist in developing the capabilities needed for the PRC to finally take them over. Japan, Taiwan and the US are in this list. In the case of India, PRC's investment of money and much else in Pakistan ensured that for a considerable period of time, there was a concentration of attention on developments concerning India's western neighbour, while the northern neighbour was not given the attention it has long merited.

Some years ago, the author developed the concept of the proxy nuclear power, which posited that a country could launch a nuclear attack on another through a proxy power that had been given the technology and ability to do so by a third power. Both the DPRK as well as Pakistan have the potential of becoming such proxy nuclear states, and both often go public about the volatile nature of the hand on the nuclear button in Pyongyang and Rawalpindi. So far as the US is concerned, it is too big and has capabilities too advanced to fear any proxies. Hence, the PRC needs to telegraph its ambitions more openly rather than remain on the sidelines of proxies, acting in a manner that seeks to degrade the security of the world's other (and still most powerful) superpower. By itself, the PRC remains far from matched with the US. However, in tandem with Russia, that distance has shrunk to a level that even those most vocal in the past about avoiding a confrontation with China are now finding impossible to ignore.

3

An Inevitable Clash of Opposing Systems

Deniers of the reality of the new cold war are still many in chancelleries, even of those countries that are most at risk from the possibility that the deepening Sino-Russian alliance will secure primacy, first over the Indo-Pacific and later over the Atlantic. One of the most influential pathways of reasoning that led many Atlanticist policymakers to this conclusion was that increasing prosperity would transform the PRC into being 'more like us' and therefore 'liking us (the Atlanticist Alliance) more'. There was a persistent belief since the end of the 1990s that, despite the 1989 Tiananmen crackdown, the CCP was communist in name only.[1] Given that several Middle Eastern allies of the Atlanticists, such as the Gulf Cooperation Council (GCC), had authoritarian governments with monopolistic power, the perception was that the economic system in China was evolving in a manner that was capitalist in all but name, and that the political system would consequently follow. Even in some countries in Europe, a few companies were indeed private, but were, in effect, controlled by the State—somewhat similar to the manner in which large private companies were subjected to multiple restrictions and prohibitions in India during the heyday of the

Soviet model in the 1960s until well into the 1980s.

In the PRC, led by a party that has, from its inception, termed itself communist, the only large companies for a considerable period were those owned by the State. In most sectors, including aviation, private players were not allowed to grow beyond a particular point. Those that did so were at risk of being taken over by the State, somewhat in the manner that domestic private banks over ₹50 crore were taken over by the Government of India in 1969. It was only during CCP General Secretary Jiang's period in office (1993–2003) that the private sector was freed of some of these constraints and encouraged to grow. Many did grow, and with the assistance of a domestic market, sheltered even after the US-assisted accession to the World Trade Organization (WTO), some became national and thereafter, global champions. However, each had to follow and keep track of the CCP directives, a few of which were made public or disseminated outside the higher portals of the Chinese 'private' companies in question. It was made mandatory for any unit employing 10 or more employees to have a CCP cell functioning within it. This cell monitored compliance with the party line.

It was small wonder that several billionaires in the PRC became members of the CCP, a fact that helped establish the myth that the PRC had a capitalist economy, albeit daubed in crimson. General Secretary Xi's period in office has led to greater transparency about the State-controlled nature of the economy, together with a similar dominance in other features of the PRC. Under Mao and his successors, the PRC became a country with a governing system that followed the ideology and practice of what may be termed 'Chinese Communism.'[2]

It was ideology that drove Cold War 1.0. The Soviet leadership were as convinced of the superiority of their philosophy of governance as US leaders were of theirs. Both were convinced that the other would enter a period of decline and collapse, and in the case of Cold War 1.0, it was the USSR that went under. It was an existential battle of systems based on conflicting ideologies, which is why those who first denied the existence, and thereafter the need for Cold War 1.0 were proved wrong. Even now, to believe that there could come a time when the foundational ideology of the Mao-Deng-Xi variant of the communist creed would be close to the governance system adopted in the US or in Western Europe is to indulge in fantasy.

The twenty-first century is nowhere close to the second half of the twentieth, and the Cold War 2.0 between the PRC and the US is as existential as its predecessor. At the close of the present contest, only one of the two systems will remain in the ring, with the other diminishing (slowly, perhaps, but steadily) into irrelevance. The CCP core is determined that unlike what happened with the USSR, in Cold War 2.0 (whose existence it repeatedly denies publicly), it will be the PRC and not the US that emerges victorious.[3] And this will be in partnership with Russia, the power that, in its earlier avatar, was vanquished by the rival system. This partnership could have been avoided had former US President Bill Clinton's administration focussed less on the next congressional mid-term elections and more on the evolving currents of history and hadn't treated the efforts made by post-USSR Moscow to put together an alliance with Washington with such contempt.

NATO AND THE MODERN COLD WAR

NATO has created a comfortable bureaucracy, where actual fighting against any significant enemy has been minimal.

Where conducted, such wars have been in conjunction with local partners (such as in Afghanistan or Iraq) that have borne the brunt of casualties. NATO and similar establishments are wary of any actions that would lead to a diminution of the financially expensive structure of privilege that they have built up, especially for the upper echelons. As a consequence of this attitude, a posting in Europe at an advanced command level in NATO is somewhat like being made the governor of a state in India. The trappings of office are far more than the effective responsibilities—if these are defined as the planning or carrying out of actual operations designed to protect and promote the security of the member states.

Had Russia been invited to join hands with NATO without being a member, it would have led to an identity crisis in the organization and among its backers. Presumably, this is one of the reasons why NATO, until the second term of the former US President Obama, acted in a manner that suggested that the USSR had not actually collapsed in 1991, but simply changed its name while shedding a few of its extremities. Russia, even under Putin, is not the USSR, and its arrival on the world stage, replacing its predecessor ought to have resulted in a similar change in Atlanticist policy.

However, bureaucracies (including think tanks that are nourished by them) resist changes in circumstances that may render their earlier strategies, personnel and machinery irrelevant. This bureaucratic resistance occurred under President Bill Clinton, and was replicated under President Biden. Interestingly, even more than under presidents Nixon or Jimmy Carter, it was during the tenure of President Clinton that the gates were thrown completely open to the PRC. This included technology transfers from the US to the PRC, unlimited entry of Chinese students into American universities and Chinese knowledge-gatherers into American research hubs.[4] However, most such avenues remained shut to India, despite its Westminster system and hundreds of millions of English language speakers that qualified the country to be a part of any twenty-first century version of the Anglosphere.

HOW THE USSR LOST COLD WAR 1.0

There is a greater possibility of a kinetic conflict between the US and the PRC than was the case between the USSR and the US. This is because of the difference between the CPSU leadership and that of the CCP. After its experience in World War II and with the passing away of Joseph Stalin in 1953, the CPSU fell into the control of careerists rather than driven ideologues. These were individuals who placed the advancement of their own careers ahead of their strategic calculations. Certainly, the promotion of the Soviet model was important, as was facing down the US in non-kinetic ways. This was because such moves, or the perception that such moves were being made, were helpful in advancing careers within the CPSU and not out of any innate hostility to the other side.

The leadership of the USSR lived in a persistent and almost paranoid fear of having their country devastated by a US first strike, and they expended much of their resources and talent on deterring such an attack. Simultaneously, the intense accretion of military powers at the cost of civilian welfare and the economy was used in a self-defeatingly parsimonious manner. An example is the 1980s conflict in Afghanistan, when the Soviet military was put in an impossible situation of trying to prevent it from expelling its conventional forces through irregular warfare. The only way to avoid defeat would have been to take the war into Pakistan, which was the staging area for the conflict and the safe zone for those engaged in fighting Soviet soldiers and airmen. Given the deterrence capability of the USSR of the time, the US would not have militarily intervened on Pakistan's side in the event of a Soviet attack on Pakistan. This could have taken the form of air attacks as well as a naval blockade. The USSR would finally have needed to declare victory in Afghanistan and abandon its efforts at converting its society into an 'Afghan Communist' model. However, had the conflict been expanded into Pakistan early on, by 1983 a respectable retreat could have been made from the maximalist goals unwisely set by CPSU General Secretary Leonid Brezhnev.

Soon after Soviet-Afghan War started, Brezhnev became physically incapacitated and the higher command of the Soviet system went into stasis. A decision as consequential as expanding the war into Pakistan was beyond the range of options that an essentially caretaker regime was capable of making. After Brezhnev died in 1982, the USSR continued to be under the nominal control of individuals whose priority was eking out a few more months of existence in the terminal state that they were in. The KGB boss Yuri Andropov may have, in his prime, understood the implications of the slowly evolving disaster in Afghanistan. However, it was not Konstantin Chernenko, the seventh general secretary of the CPSU, but Andropov who spent what little energy he had left on working out ways to ensure that a new leadership formed after his passing, rather than spending time on a campaign that he had left to his generals. They expectedly carried out activities solely at a tactical level, when the only way out of the quagmire would have been in strategic shifts in Soviet military action—shifts that the terminally ill Andropov was incapable of making. The ailing Andropov groomed a favourite—Mikhail Gorbachev—

who took over as the CPSU general secretary in 1985.

From 1985, Cold War 1.0 was lost, and not just that contest, but the USSR itself was lost. A system that had based its security on domestic and international fear generated by the capabilities of its military and security agency had come under the control of a leader like Gorbachev, who was a votary of abjuring force in any form and who oversaw the regime-destroying and humiliating withdrawal of the Soviet occupation forces from Afghanistan in 1989. By that time, taking advantage of the votary of non-violence who was heading the most ferocious war machine in the world, Eastern Europe declared its freedom from Soviet control and the collapse of the USSR followed. Gorbachev was surprised by this event.[5] This was not surprising for an individual who expected those who were implacably opposed to the Soviet system—such as the leadership in the US and in western Europe, and who were committed to its downfall—to generously assist the USSR.

It is another matter that the US and its Atlanticist allies made the situation in Afghanistan even worse than the muddle that Soviet forces had left behind. This happened because of their backing for Pashtun religious extremists—rather than moderate but nationalistic Pashtuns—to take control of Afghanistan. In 1996, President Clinton capped this policy by getting the Taliban installed in Afghanistan—the opposite of an achievement. This was repeated by President Biden in 2021, this time not in response to the views of the energy industry in the US (represented ably in matters dealing with Afghanistan by Zalmay Khalilzad, the US special representative for Afghanistan reconciliation), but for domestic political reasons. Of course, the US being prepared to concede defeat even to the Taliban had the opposite effect of what Biden had wanted, not just in domestic politics but in the confidence of the US's allies in Asia that it was a reliable partner against the PRC's expansionism.

TREADING ON AMERICAN TOES

The CCP leadership core analysed the reality of the decline and fall of the USSR more comprehensively and closely than scholars elsewhere.[6] The moribund nature of the Soviet economy had become impossible to conceal by the close of the 1970s and it only became worse during the 1980s. In place of the USSR's strategy of geopolitically challenging the US, Deng bided his time and hid his objective to reinstate the PRC as the Middle Kingdom. From then onwards, the PRC embarked on a period of economic reform that converted a backward economy into a global commercial hub. Deng may have worn Stetson hats and walked around with cowboy boots while on a visit to the US, but under the hat, the Paramount Leader was unchanged in his belief in the innate superiority of the CCP system of governance and in the correctness, indeed necessity, of the CCP's drive to achieve the PRC's Middle Kingdom objective.

Had the Great Proletarian Cultural Revolution not taken place, it may have proved impossible for Paramount Leader Deng to have pushed through the transformative policy changes that he implemented as the leader of the CCP. The Cultural Revolution not only weakened but also destroyed much of the senior leadership of the CCP, and Deng was among the very few elders standing by the time the process ended. Consequently, he was able to push through policy changes, such as the welcoming of foreign investment, despite frowns from traditionalists who had been steeped in the doctrine that such reforms were a symptom of the 'capitalist road.' Deng followed the road that he believed was essential to the PRC's rise, and if capitalism with CCP characteristics could increase the speed of progress, so be it. In that sense, Deng had the same objective as the other two foundational leaders of the CCP—Mao and Xi—the rise of the PRC to global primacy, except that their methods have sometimes differed.

Since 2012, the year in which he assumed the role of captaining one of the world's superpowers, Xi has moved away from Mao in terms of his outreach to the roots of Chinese civilization (parts of which were regarded with contempt for having kept China weak for centuries). He has also moved away from Deng's policy of keeping the stick of the PLA—which has been growing bigger and bigger since around the time of the handover of Hong Kong in 1997—concealed. Instead, the PLA has been made the centrepiece even of much of PRC diplomacy. Xi, in particular, has put the PLA at the centre of much of China's external messaging, while Deng had sought to conceal or underplay the military in his own diplomacy in the 1980s, a trend that continued with Jiang and Hu. The PLA, in its various formations, is joining hands with partners and expanding its areas of interest and effectiveness. In this context, the manner in which Xi has concretized the Sino-Russian alliance has become a force multiplier for both countries, but especially for the PRC.

Judging by his actions and statements, it is clear that Xi is in agreement with those who argue that the US is in a period of decline that seems difficult to even slow down, much less halt and reverse. The ways in which the US's soft and hard powers (especially the latter) have been deployed to secure and advance US interests have been studied, and several of these methods are being adopted by Xi (with Chinese Communist characteristics). This is similar to the way Deng sought to replicate aspects of the US manufacturing model in China while adjusting to local conditions, including political ones. Deng made it clear to former British PM Margret Thatcher that Britain would have to exit Hong Kong and could not retain even a residue of its former control over the territory. Thus, Deng was cautious about treading on the toes of Washington, unlike London, whose toes he stomped on in the Hong Kong issue. Xi has not been as reticent as Deng. The calculation is that the deliberately visible rise in the offensive capabilities of the PRC would sufficiently deter the US (and even more so, a lesser power) from obstructing the PRC's drive towards 'reclaiming' territory, including the areas that existed only in the maps of the Middle Kingdom, if even in that. Xi was heartened by Obama's period in office since he made the same symbolic advances against the PRC military as President Clinton had in the past. However, he did nothing tangible when Beijing took over Scarborough Shoal from the Philippines and began reinforcing its position in the South China Sea. Such expansion of territory by the Chinese side slowed down somewhat during the Trump administration. Should President Biden follow the precedent set by presidents Clinton and Obama, and generate much sound and fury without any accompanying fire, such moves will accelerate during his term in office. Given the security imperatives of the US, it would be counter-productive if President Biden took a soft touch approach towards the PRC that many believe he will. Such a view has not dimmed after President Biden's 2022 pivot back to the Atlantic from the Indo-Pacific, and to the familiarity and convenience of having Moscow as the prime enemy rather than Beijing.

Being at the top of the food chain carries significant ancillary benefits, hence the focus by the CCP leadership on the PRC replacing the US as the world's largest economy by conventional calculations. The PRC overtaking Japan as the bigger economy had an immediate impact on the power dynamics between East and Southeast Asia, and on Japan itself. Certainly, the mood in the PRC was that a country that had not very long ago occupied and ravaged several parts of China had finally got its comeuppance. It also helped strengthen the bonds of obedience and, to an extent, appreciation that the average PRC citizen had towards the CCP. After all, this was the party that had made the PRC not only a huge geographic entity, but also an economic wunderkind. Should the PRC overtake the US during General Secretary Xi's period in office, it would greatly help the CCP leadership ensure the continued acceptance of the inevitability of its rule among the Chinese people.

CHINA: RULING WITH FEAR AND RESPECT

Fear and respect are the twin drivers of fealty to a regime among a people, with affection for it being a distant third. In USSR, the respect towards the regime evaporated when Nikita Khruschev, the former premier of the USSR, in his secret speech to the 20th Congress of the CPSU in 1956, revealed the misdeeds of Joseph Stalin. The contents of this secret speech did not remain so from the people of USSR for very long. Through samizdat newsletters and other ways, including effective dissemination by US agencies, the contents of the speech were widely available by the end of the 1960s. Much of its contents were already known to the Soviet population, just as what Adolf Hitler was doing in the concentration camps during World War II was known among the German population. However, the fact that it was the General Secretary of the CPSU who revealed some of the ugliest truths of the Stalinist period convinced tens of millions in the USSR that the CPSU leadership was rotten at the core. Earlier, they had been told that the hardships and injustices they had endured had been necessary to succeed in the war against German invaders, whose depravity overshadowed even the misdeeds of Stalin and his henchmen. That fig leaf was removed by Khruschev's secret speech. Mikhail Gorbachev ostentatiously abjured the use of force both internally and externally. During his period in office, the fear also evaporated from the Soviet system, and from then onwards, the dissolution of the USSR became inevitable.

Examining the domestic consequences of Khruschev's speech persuaded even the most strident critics (within party councils) of Mao to put aside any public examination of the impact of some of his actions and policies against not just his colleagues and the CCP but the entirety of the population of the PRC. The worry is that any such reassessment of the life and legacy of the Great Helmsman would not merely confuse the party cadres but also dilute the respect that the people of the country have for the CCP and its repeatedly presented history of struggle for the cause of a China rising from the trough of oppression by foreign powers. That 'mistakes' were made by Mao is impossible to deny, but these have been explained away as being of far less import than the many good things that he is considered to have accomplished. Certainly, the expansion of the PRC's territorial boundaries has been most significant, as compared to those of earlier empires. There is also a sense of nationalism—albeit with a Han imprint—that has, to a considerable extent, overcome regional differences and earlier prejudices. And there is, once again, a sense of mission and confidence within the Chinese people that was absent during the period in between the fall of the emperors and the setting up of the PRC. Amid all this, Mao's legendary status has been an important factor. Discrediting him in the manner that Stalin was denounced in the USSR in 1956 would affect the entire narrative of the CCP and reduce its overall acceptance and credibility among the Chinese people.

This is one of the reasons why there is a substantial body of work outside China that has meticulously documented the mishaps and tragedies that befell it during Mao's period in office (1949-76). There have even been salacious revelations about the private life of the founding Chairman of the CCP and about the famines, persecution, economic stagnation and dislocation that characterized his period in office, many disseminated within the PRC by agencies outside the country.[7] Until a future general secretary of the CCP rises to denounce Mao to the party faithful, in the manner that Khrushchev denounced Stalin, a shift in loyalties against Mao is unlikely. Both Deng as well as Xi underwent hardships during the Cultural Revolution, and both have been respectful of Mao's legacy, especially Xi. Indeed, in a way, what has emerged as Xi Jinping Thought is an amalgam of Mao Zedong Thought and Lin Biao Thought, mixed with generous doses of classical Chinese texts and history. Given its intellectual and ideological DNA, it is inevitable that the drive to attain primacy over the US will continue under Xi. The logic behind his actions, thus far, vindicates the perception that the General Secretary, even on his rare conciliatory moments, follows Mao's maxim of 'retreat when the enemy advances', and advance again 'when the enemy retreats' through smart policy. The PRC's policy has been literally 'smart', as AI has been given a cornerstone role in the development of its military capability.

THE FRONTS FOR CHINESE EXPANSION

Short of giving the PRC a walkover in the global primacy sweepstakes, and facing its attendant consequences on the US system but its internal salience, the US administration has no other option but to accept the logic of Cold War 2.0 and try to prevent Beijing from claiming the space that it wants and getting Washington to vacate it. No US president or general secretary of the CCP would like to follow in the footsteps of Gorbachev. This shared resolve has made the ongoing contest between the two superpowers inevitable. In the present phase of the effort to expand the footprint and control of the PRC over others, there are three likely fronts that could be activated in a kinetic manner—the Himalayan massif, the South China Sea and the Taiwan straits.

The CCP has already secured a strong position across the Himalayan massif, including its control of what is now the Tibet Autonomous Region (TAR) and other regions that were once part of Tibet but which have since been divested from it. Complete control over the Himalayan massif would involve—over a phased period—control over the northern and southern borders of Nepal and Bhutan, and the takeover of sufficient additional territory in Ladakh, and would render any effort by India to reclaim its earlier territorial assets inoperative. Control over the massif would give Beijing control over the water resources that are needed by countries to its south, as well as a possible source of additional water supplies reaching up to its industrial and commercial heartland on its east coast.

By establishing its dominance over the South China Sea, the PRC would gain control over a waterway that is critical to much of the trade passing between East and Southeast Asia, and other parts of the world. It would undo the control of the powers that are obstacles to the primacy of the PRC over the US over maritime choke points, giving that control to Beijing instead. The waters of the South China Sea would be a plentiful source of minerals and other resources, which would be necessary for a country with a higher growth trajectory than what has been already established as its record for the speed and extent of its economic progress. 'Socialism with Chinese Communist characteristics in one country' is at the heart of policy in the PRC. This is being defined as the continuation of the CCP's power and the perpetuation of a governance system in which the control levers for all sections of society and activity are in the hands of its leadership.

The third area of interest, which is at a level that may lead to conflict, is Taiwan. General Secretary Xi is looking to his place in history, and for this to be suitably burnished, what is needed is the unification of Taiwan with the PRC. This is an objective that has not remained hidden at any time since the establishment of the PRC in 1949, and was explicitly mentioned in the 1971 discussions that led to the partnership between Washington and Beijing to weaken the influence and stability of Moscow. These objectives are aligned with the overall goal of replacing Washington with Beijing at the centre of global policy, and are considered to be promoting this outcome, as indeed they would, were they to happen.

WHY RUSSIA LEANS TOWARDS CHINA

It is not a surprise that the PRC of Xi and Russia of Putin have become increasingly interlocked into a security alliance that is mutually beneficial. Both are revivalists, with Xi taking forward the 'China Dream' of enthroning the PRC as the Middle Kingdom once again, and Putin getting back the influence and global heft that the USSR possessed in its heyday. In that sense, Putin is more like Mao, who shunned the 'olds' as having been responsible for the eventual decline and downfall of China. The seemingly permanent ruler of Russia is no admirer of the Tsarist system, and hence, depictions of him as 'Tsar Putin' may elicit a wry smile from him. Rather, he is the vozhd, the supreme leader that Stalin turned out to be, who will bring Russia back from the brink as the dictator did in his time and make his country a superpower again because it has the potential to be one.

Relations between Russia and western powers have fluctuated since World War II. Stalin recognized that the coming to power of Hitler in a country of the size and sophistication of Germany meant that Moscow needed to combine with London and Paris, no matter what their past differences had been. The Nazi-Soviet pact of 1939 was the default option, reluctantly adopted by the USSR only after the UK and France effectively scorned the offer of an alliance with the USSR to establish a mechanism of collective security against what Stalin (and Churchill) were sure would be tides of war launched by the German Fuehrer.

It was fortunate for Britain that Churchill—and not Edward Frederick Lindley Wood—First Earl of Halifax, commonly known as Lord Halifax—was appointed the PM by Conservative Party Members of Parliament (MPs) after it became clear that Neville Chamberlain, the former PM of the UK, had to go. In large part, this was because neither the country, as a whole, nor the Labour Party would favour an aristocrat whose propensity for appeasing Hitler had been amply demonstrated in his past actions. More than the Conservative MPs—a majority of whom disliked Churchill intensely—it was the Labour Party leadership of the time that forced Churchill into 10 Downing Street as a precondition for joining a national government to fight a war that was going very badly at the time and for a considerable period afterwards. Had Halifax been the PM rather than Churchill, it is likely that Whitehall would have sought an accommodation with the Fuehrer rather than allying with Stalin in the way Churchill did. There do not seem to be any more Roosevelts or Churchills in Washington and London, at least until now.

Stalin chose to accommodate with Germany when Britain and France under PM Chamberlain and PM Édouard Daladier respectively, gave him no alternative. In much the same fashion, the Atlantic powers, in a partnership newly invigorated by President Biden's shift in focus back to the Atlantic and Russia, are leaving no option for Putin but to accept the alliance with the PRC, even though the objective of Beijing is to comprehensively replace Russia as the predominant power in Eurasia.

Given the lack of options of Russia and President Putin, and the use of Atlanticist-created fault lines by CCP General Secretary Xi, they fit as strong allies, as do the countries led by them. There is no way that a Russia led by Putin, which therefore, insists on reclaiming most of the rights and privileges it had in the days before President Boris Yeltsin's tenure, would be likely to work out a mutually acceptable accommodation with the member states of NATO or with the EU as a whole. Even Yeltsin—with all the destructive compromises he made—could not engineer such a collaborative outcome. There is no way that a PRC led by Xi—who has put the recreation of China as the Middle Kingdom in his policies—would be able to fashion a mutually acceptable settlement with the US and its allies to reduce tensions, and ensure a return to the days of Deng and Jiang. Unless one or the other side surrenders its interests and objectives in a fashion that seems unlikely, almost impossible, at present, the Cold War 2.0 will continue.

4

The Indispensable Indo-Pacific Partner

It is indispensable for the Sino-Russian alliance that India does not join the US in the task of ensuring a free and open Indo-Pacific instead of being the theatre of war where major choke points, such as the South China Sea and the first island chain in the East China Sea, are dominated by the rival US-led alliance. India is a crucial partner to the US if Washington is to prevail over the efforts of Beijing, which is being assisted by Moscow, to establish domination over the Indo-Pacific before moving on to the Atlantic. Such a shift by Beijing will happen once the Indo-Pacific is secured from the primacy of the Indo-pacific Freedom Alliance, especially in the military sphere.

The Sino-Russian partnership, while working jointly on securing primacy in both the waters, is designed to ensure that the lead role in the Indo-Pacific (once secured) is played by Beijing. The problem for Russia is that its goal of similarly dominating the Atlantic is not shared by its closest partner, the PRC. General Secretary Xi would like to ensure this for his own country—not for Russia. However, given the disappointing post-Cold War 1.0 trajectory, even a grandmaster of geopolitical chess, such as Putin, may not be able to prevent such an outcome because there is an absence of a strategy with Russia that resembles the Nixon strategy with the PRC (i.e. creating an alliance designed to weaken the main challenge, which in Cold War 2.0 is no longer Russia but China).

OPPORTUNITIES AS THE ROUTE TO POWER

Given the absence of a shift in the American strategy, the Sino-Russian alliance is likely to last for the decades to come. Both Xi and Putin have carefully studied the rise of the US and the attendant belief in American exceptionalism, and they are believers of a similar Chinese and Russian exceptionalism, respectively. The departments analysing world events that serve the leadership core of the CCP have exhaustively studied the historical pathways through which the UK and, later, the US established their primacy over the globe. They have also looked into how the US overcame the challenges they faced in the trajectory leading up to the achievement of this primacy. European empires and their creation have been a staple of study in training schools for CCP cadres.[1] The problem for Xi particularly is that hypotheses about the rise of British and, later, US domination may err in assuming a master strategy or a bouquet of such strategies. Their trajectory may not have involved any pre-planned and systematic strategy to achieve the goal of global primacy. Their leadership may have had the will and comprehension to take advantage of opportunities that assisted their climb to the top.

PM Churchill, more than any of his senior colleagues in the Conservative Party of the time, is said to have had the will and the confidence to challenge Germany under Hitler, when it seemed to be on an almost effortless journey towards global primacy and domination over many of the territories affected by such expansionism. Furthermore, Churchill even understood the essentiality of a partnering with the USSR to defeat Germany. The American voters had the good fortune of electing Abraham Lincoln as president, who kept the US united, albeit at the cost of a bloody war with the Confederacy. In the 1930s, it was again the good fortune of US voters that they ensured the entry and continued stay of Franklin Roosevelt in the White House. He was an individual who understood that the social fabric of the US was in danger of unravelling unless the underprivileged were served justice. He later also displayed the foresight and clarity needed to confront Hitler along with other countries that had been threatened by the German dictator. Few of Roosevelt's peers in the political leadership of the US at the time saw the developing situation in Europe with as much acuity as he did.

In India, the leaders of the INC accepted Partition in 1947, unlike Netaji Subhas Chandra Bose, who may not have done this, had he been leading the INC at the time. Over the decades, India has had multiple opportunities for riding a geopolitical wave that would have aided the interests of the country—these opportunities were squandered. Even after Independence, India has been a country blessed with a vibrant population and a surfeit of opportunities for advancement. Yet, for long periods of time, it has remained shackled by the inability or unwillingness of the leadership of the day to take advantage of such opportunities.

The parable of an individual facing punishment in the form of consuming a cupful of salt or a receiving a hundred lashes of the whip is well known. The unfortunate individual took some salt, then decided that he preferred the whip. After a few lashes, he again returned to the salt. Ultimately, he finished almost all the salt and was administered all the lashes. Similarly, foreign policy in India has been designed to minimize the risk of 'punishment', should it become inescapable. Soft options with hard consequences have been a common feature of Indian foreign policy.

During Cold War 1.0, the choices made by the political leadership of India and implemented by the foreign service ensured that between the 1950s and 1980s, the country suffered from the consequences of having the worst of both worlds. The economy suffered due to statist policies. On the foreign policy front, the western world regarded India as too pro-Soviet to assist its economic progress. This was in contrast to their assistance of Pakistan through defence and other supplies, based on a treaty of allyship between Pakistan and the West. This lack of favour among the West was a consequence of India shying away from an alliance with the US, while energetically seeking partnerships with a country like the PRC, which had no interest in a strong, stable India ever emerging. Even in the pre-1959 days of *Hindi-Chini Bhai Bhai*, Aksai Chin had been occupied. Action after action (if not words and statements) showed that Beijing saw New Delhi as a rival that needed to be put in its place and kept there.

INDO-RUSSIAN FRIENDSHIP

It must be said that the Soviet leadership understood the importance of keeping India away from the US-led alternative and went the extra mile in meeting India's industrial and defence needs, intervening where necessary in the UNSC, among other ways. This was a strategic relationship that was more than transactional. The US, on the contrary, has been superficial, which is why the administration of the ultra-transactional President Trump[2] lacked credibility in its offers of partnership with potential allies. Once Trump became the

US president, Vice-President Mike Pence, the National Security Council and the US Department of State, headed by Mike Pompeo, understood the necessity of getting India into the US's corner. They knew that this would open up a treasure trove of opportunities to constrain and finally contain China. The opportunities they provided were often not taken advantage of by the Indian side, which was focussed on remaining ambiguous about its geopolitical preferences. The USSR had understood the significance of enmeshing India within its defence production net in such a way that all three services became dependent on Moscow for much of their firepower and reach. This situation had come about when Moscow had started being hostile to Beijing and vice versa. It was expected that the dependence on what was now Russia for defence imports would need to be lessened, but this has only been happening in the recent past.[3]

Had the US administration under President Clinton responded in the manner that the Pentagon did under Obama's, and even more so, during Trump's presidency, Washington may have replaced Moscow as India's primary partner, once the USSR disintegrated in 1991. Unfortunately, during almost all of President Clinton's time in office, the US obsessively focussed on trying to ensure the continuation of the PRC's nuclear monopoly in Asia by seeking to deprive India of not just the domestic ability to make nuclear weapons but also nuclear electricity. Clinton also sought to reward the extremist-reliant military in Pakistan by trying to force PM Narasimha Rao to make concessions in Kashmir that would have ended India's control over the defence and security of that state, allowing it to slide into Rawalpindi's grip.[4]

INDIAN CONCESSIONS, FOREIGN ASSURANCES

Israel's security and interests have often been boosted due to the Palestine Liberation Organization's (PLO) leadership refusing to accept concessions that were less than the (unrealistic) minimum that the Palestinian leadership was demanding. The concessions made by Israel over time were usually rejected. In practically every such situation, Israel benefitted due to a departure from the ground realities of the Palestinian side, which erred in ways that harmed the interests of the Palestinians.[5]

In a similar fashion, had the leadership in Pakistan possessed the wisdom to accept the concessions on Kashmir that were being offered by the Indian side in the 1990s, and later, in the initial years of the twenty-first century, under pressure from the US, they would have strengthened their position even in Kashmir. However, Pakistan persistently adopted the approach that the PRC had successfully done several times with India—pocketing concessions, and when they became irreversible, abandoning its own obligations under any agreement, or understanding and demanding even more concessions.[6] This is why the Line of Actual Control (LAC) has been shifting to India's disadvantage for a considerable period of time, although this is seldom highlighted by the Indian side, perhaps out of worry of an adverse public reaction.[7] It was the belief within the uniformed leadership of Pakistan that by holding out, they could get more of the concessions that President Clinton, or some of his successors, had demanded from India, rather than the significant but limited advantages offered to them by New Delhi. These offers from New Delhi were a consequence of what can only be described as harassment and intimidation, especially by the Clinton administration, which made as little secret of its tilt towards Pakistan as was done earlier by Nixon and Kissinger during the Bangladesh Liberation War.[8]

Another opportunity was presented to Pakistan in the form of the concessions offered by an 'unofficial envoy' to Pakistan during the Vajpayee administration. These concessions were reiterated even after Pervez Musharraf, the chief martial law administrator, took over the reins of governance from then PM Nawaz Sharif in 1999. The canny Musharraf had fully understood the benefits of adopting the PRC model of accepting one-sided concessions and subsequently, not reciprocating but demanding more. General Musharraf came to Agra in 2001 to implement such a strategy, only to find that Home Minister L.K. Advani and Defence Minister George Fernandes had succeeded in persuading PM Vajpayee to not implement the numerous concessions offered by the 'unofficial envoy.'[9] Essentially, India's talks with Pakistan followed the Shimla model of 1972, in which India made substantive concessions and in exchange, received only vague assurances of future goodwill.[10] Chasing the media headlines created by such vaporous assurances from Pakistan has been a characteristic of the Indian political leadership. Too many of the country's leaders have gone from spin to spin, from headline to headline.

RUSSIA OVER AMERICA AND ITS CONSEQUENCES

Early in his tenure, Finance Minister (FM) Manmohan Singh, with the approval of PM Narasimha Rao, decided to agree to an artificially high level for the Russian rouble to repay debts that were outstanding for the purchase of Soviet weaponry.[11] The wisdom, or lack thereof, in this decision is yet to be sufficiently examined. No other country followed this profligate example, nor was it necessary. Russia was desperate for foreign exchange, and the sales of weaponry to India would have continued even if the 1993 rupee–rouble arrangement had not been signed. Had India's leaders internalized the imperative of safeguarding the interests of the people of India rather than that of outside powers or narrow bands of vested interests within the country, the rupee–rouble arrangement of 1993 would never have been signed. This concession involved additional payments, over time, of more than $10 billion. It was, in effect, a form of foreign aid from a much poorer India to Russia. The deal delighted the Clinton administration, which may have leveraged its support to Russia to secure more concessions from President Yeltsin, of course, not for New Delhi, but for Washington. Apart from a few stray mentions, what represents an abandonment of the national interest in favour of a foreign power has hardly been commented upon, much less criticized.

The stated intention behind the agreement was to ensure continuous supply of Russian weaponry and systems to India. It is worth reiterating that this was something that would have happened regardless, given the need for the Russian defence production industry to grab as many markets as possible during the chaos of the Yeltsin years. As for the Russian President, he followed Gorbachev's obsessive focus on trying to improve the relations with the US and major EU nations. The response of the US and the EU was warm in words but cold in practice, similar to what India had endured with the PRC. It must be said that the USSR remained the only technological power that was able and willing to assist India during the period when the US was committed to backing an army-run Pakistan, even to the extent of ignoring the manner in which the PRC was creating the nuclear and missile capability of Pakistan during the Carter–Reagan period.

Clinton and his immediate successors in the White House apparently believed that Pakistan's PRC-gifted nuclear capability was an advantage, in that India would get so alarmed by this, and consent to a mutual elimination of its nuclear and missile programmes, on the condition that Pakistan did the same. Those were the days when the non-proliferation lobbies in the US and China worked closely together against a single target—not Pakistan, not North Korea, but India. Despite PM Narasimha Rao signalling his readiness to enter into a relationship with the US to replace India's relationship with the USSR, which had for long been its principal backer in the UN, the Clinton administration refused to carry forward a partnership that had been on the minds of US presidents who had a sense of history and understood the influence of such an alliance on geopolitics, like John Kennedy.

The influence of a section of British administration—which had previously exerted a similar influence on Nehru—ensured that Washington and New Delhi steadily drifted apart from each other. This happened despite a congruence of core interests between India and the US, even during the 1950s, which Sardar Patel would have appreciated and sought to act upon, had he not passed away at the beginning of the decade. For quite a while, the US saw India as a model that could demonstrate its superiority against the Communist Chinese model, and good relations between Washington and New Delhi would have sped up the process of India's development.

The 1960s were a period of internal flux in India, and the USSR proved to be a stable and reliable partner at a time when the US and the UK were still looking to Pakistan as their most reliable ally in South Asia. Indeed, this may have been the UK's reason to support the creation of an independent Pakistan in 1947. Delhi's strident tone of opposition to the Vietnam War (morally correct though it was) ensured that the relationship between Washington and New Delhi remained strained into the 1960s, despite breakthroughs such as the Green Revolution, where US expertise was invaluable in securing a modicum of food security for India. Food and Agriculture Minister C. Subramaniam was responsible for implementing the 1964–67 Green Revolution that had begun during the prime ministership of Shastri and was further continued by his successor, Indira Gandhi.

In the 1970s, the relationship between China and the US flowered. This knocked out the primary strategic rationale—competing with China and balancing the influence of Beijing—for greater US involvement in India's efforts at growth. Instead, Washington became the principal enabler of the rise of PRC influence and economic progress, a situation that continued into the 1980s, until the final couple of years in office of CPSU General Secretary Gorbachev. By that time, it had become obvious to many (although not to Gorbachev himself, who clung on to his illusions to the end of his tenure) that the USSR was on the way to the meltdown that finally came at the close of Gorbachev's term in 1991.

By the time Tiananmen Square was cleared of protestors in 1989, the PRC had reached a level where it did not need any external crutches to grow, but could do so provided that the overall environment for expansion of its trade was benign, which it largely was. Only with President Bush coming to power in 2001 did those who had been warning of the eventual consequences of the expansion of Chinese power since the early 1990s, including individuals like Richard Fisher, find resonance in the White House. But the US's focus on China did not survive 9/11. After that, attention shifted away from China to Afghanistan and the Middle East and remained that way until the final years of the Obama administration, during the period when Ashton Carter was the secretary of defence (2015–17). During this period, the move away from an Atlanticist focus to an Indo-Pacific focus was initiated, a change in policy continued and reinforced during the Trump presidency (2017–21), which may be in the danger of being upended by President Biden in 2022.

TWO CONFLICTING BLOCS

Any viable strategy of retaining US primacy over the Indo-Pacific needs to be aided by India, Japan, Australia and, in time, Indonesia. At the same time, the PRC needs to ensure that India stays away from any formal or even tacit military alliance with the US, and in trying to ensure this, continues to rely heavily on the goodwill that Moscow has long had in New Delhi, a capital where much of the differentiation between the USSR and Russia has been lost in translation. This difference was as stark between the Yeltsin–Gorbachev duo and earlier leaders in Moscow, where the importance of India within the web of global relationships of the then superpower was understood.

Currently, the Association of Southeast Asian Nations (ASEAN) needs to understand the scale of the present and future opportunities that would be lost to its members were they to abide by a Beijing-drafted 'Code of Conduct' for some of the waters of the Indo-Pacific. Such a code would legitimize the rising degree of control of Beijing over the waters of the South China Sea. Even if ASEAN, as a collective, agrees to such a humiliating and self-limiting condition, powers such as Japan, Australia and India would not, and neither would most of the countries from the EU. Just as the South China Sea does not belong to the PRC, it does not belong to the member-states of ASEAN either, and hence is not theirs to dispose of.

Xi Jinping Thought posits that any individual of Han descent is duty bound to assist the CCP in its grand strategy of re-establishing the PRC as the Middle Kingdom. The ethnic Chinese diaspora across the world, including in Southeast Asia, is expected to place themselves at the service of the CCP leadership core in its plans for the countries of which they are citizens. While some have done so, others have hesitated or declined, aware that loyalty to a country other than that of which they are citizens could be problematic in future. In a world where there is, once again, an open contest between two superpowers, the business community, in particular, is likely to have to choose between one bloc or the other in case they are involved in the manufacture and distribution of dual use technologies. In an era when AI is expanding its scope, this includes a broad swathe of products, such as online applications and telecom. Strategic planners in the PRC have taken care to ensure that lightly policed fields of online activity worldwide, such as online gaming, have steadily been taken over by entities controlled by the PRC.[12]

Such control over the data streams generated by internet platforms and mobile applications has given the PLA and associated security agencies access to information about the personality characteristics of different segments of a population,[13] including the triggers that fuel anger or generate hate[14]. The use of social media platforms to send across carefully crafted messaging, designed to increase the depth and extent of such emotions, has been developed by special units within the PLA, which is increasingly working alongside the Russian military as well as with subsidiary partners such as GHQ Rawalpindi.[15] Any major conflict would, therefore, involve an attack on the home front, and Cold War 2.0 is being fought in this manner.

PROBLEMS FACED BY LARGE DEMOCRACIES

In any democracy, once fringe (as distinct from more moderate) groups of the Right and the Left expand within the population—as they have been doing in the two largest democracies in the world, India and the US—societal stability comes under threat of eruptions of violence. Each such threat poses a risk to the idea of democracy, which mandates an amicable and, therefore, broadly equitable settlement of differences between competing sides.

India and the US are both facing similar threats. These include terrorism, efforts at the expansion of influence by authoritarian states and internal dissensions that are often substantially fuelled from outside, especially through the use of social media platforms. The advantages that the US brings to the table are obvious. They include the availability of a hitherto unmatched range of weapons systems and technologies. India brings with it the advantage of a limitless supply of manpower that can be harnessed to defend itself and its allies. To tap this source of strength, a programme that provides national service training involving tens of millions of youths needs to be established in India, so that the rigour associated with such a regimen would instil within its participants a sense of devotion and fealty to serving the national interest. At present, because of the lack of such schemes, millions of youths are at risk of falling victim to the snares of those domestic and foreign entities that seek to utilize them to cause mayhem in the streets. This would ostensibly be in the cause of some of the issues of the day, but, in reality, would be carried out simply to cause disruption designed to derail efforts at growth and its consequent benefits to social stability.

The best-case scenario for the Sino-Russian alliance would

be that India remains outside the system of partnerships being designed to frustrate the efforts of this alliance to establish primacy over the waters of the Indo-Pacific. For the PRC, during President Biden's term, the best-case would be if India distances itself from the Cold War 2.0 deniers (especially those who remain in thrall to the unreal assumption that it is the Atlantic rather than the Indo-Pacific that is the global centre of gravity or that it should be). Within the Biden administration, there are many who seek to focus the attention of the White House on domestic foes and Russia rather than on the PRC having become by far the principal threat to US interests and primacy worldwide. This is most visible in the way in which NATO, led by the US, has allowed its attention to be diverted from the Indo-Pacific back to the Atlantic and to factors in Russia as *the* enemy, rather than the actual challenger, which is the PRC. In domestic politics, the Biden administration is going after Trump supporters, forgetting that Russia, China and Wahhabi interests are actively promoting hate within the US society, mainly through online forums and messaging. The external enemy is real, and needs much more attention than domestic political rivals. Should Biden's focus once again shift to the Indo-Pacific, in the manner that was first witnessed during the final years of the Obama presidency and continued under Trump, and should India abandon its continuing hesitations in coming to a robust security relationship with the US, the partnership thus formed would almost certainly prevail in Cold War 2.0—a contest now being played out over multiple fronts, including the seas, space, society, health and online.

Both the Indian Ocean rim as well as the Himalayan massif are critical to the security of India, and both are under threat of being dominated by China—a superpower that has for long been in a force multiplier relationship with GHQ Rawalpindi through its own military. The Sino-Pakistan alliance has neither succeeded in weakening India to any appreciable degree, nor in constraining New Delhi from exercising influence within South Asia, especially when it is severely challenged, as has been the case with Nepal or the Maldives in recent years. A strengthened defence and security relationship between the US and India is as much an imperative for the former as it is for the latter, notwithstanding the distractions caused by the side issues dear to the hearts of the GHQ Rawalpindi or PRC lobbies in the Washington Beltway being attended to. To keep the focus of the Biden administration on such issues, rather than developing a policy matrix based on the Great Game, is the objective of the PLA with its proxy in Pakistan.

COLLABORATING WITH THE US

There is the 'small game' and the 'little game', and countries that lose out in geopolitical contests are those which prioritize the latter rather than focussing on the Great Game being played by rival powers, especially in a contest between superpowers. Relations between countries have to be judged in the context of the ongoing effort by Russia, China and a few extreme religious dispensations that work in concert with the PRC to displace the primacy of the US and its partners (including India). It is important to douse the bush fires ignited by hostile players in the Great Game of exchanging the unipolar world order that had long been dominated by the US with its PRC equivalent. However, the tactics used for this need to be synchronized with an overall strategy to ensure the unity of the two biggest democracies in all situations where their mutual interests converge. This includes the freedom of the Indo-Pacific from being controlled by a hostile power and cracking down on terrorist networks. However, this synchronized strategy does not work in a situation when the US seeks, based on its obsession with Ukraine, to shift its focus once again to Russia and Europe, in the process, neglecting dealing with China and the Asian three-fourths of Eurasia.

To avoid this trap, it would be essential for the Biden administration to have India on its side to implement not simply skilful diplomacy but also practical measures of collaboration, especially in the fields of defence and security. We need to have an alliance not of Five Eyes but of Seven Eyes. India and Japan need to join Australia, Canada, New Zealand, the UK and the US, which have evolved into multiracial entities, rather than being limited to the variety celebrated not only by Hitler but also by the Enoch Powells and the Stephen Millers of the world.

In the past, the US has recognized the importance of India in various fields. While allowing US-made pharmaceutical products to monopolize, in the Trump way, the Bush administration recognized that the objective of reducing the threat of HIV/AIDS to tens of millions of African lives could only be achieved by ensuring a comprehensive partnership with India.[16] The only way that Vermont Senator Bernie Sanders can get the universal healthcare that he seeks at an affordable cost to the US taxpayer is to involve healthcare professionals and providers from India in this effort. Similarly, in the field of nuclear fusion and energy, the US collaborating with India could achieve effective results in a much faster manner than if the two countries worked alone.

The US and India are already working together in many areas of science and technology as a consequence of the involvement of Indian-Americans and others of Indian origin, who are working in the US or for it. Many citizens regarded as being lower down the food chain by the bureaucracy in India (which, of course, believes itself to be the final arbiter of all activity) have already decided, with their airline tickets and collaborations, that the US and India should be partners in such fields, either by moving there or working for US entities. The government needs to catch up with rather than seek to hold such people back. Although, this is what could happen if the Government of India continues to send confusing signals, especially in a period when Cold War 2.0 has become an inescapable reality.

Just as the Sino-Russian alliance is an unfortunate reality, so too is the PLA's support to the ambitions of GHQ Rawalpindi in Kashmir and Ladakh. This support has not even been concealed from May 2020 onwards.[17] The effort by Islamabad, Beijing and Moscow to prevent a future India–US defence and security partnership remains a work in progress rather than an objective that has failed. As long as this is the case, the vulnerability of the 1.38 billion people of the Republic of India to a discernible external shock of a kinetic nature and to infiltration of mindspace through social media discourse remains high, as does the vulnerability of the primacy of the US-led alliance in the Indo-Pacific.

RUSSIAN FRIENDSHIP A SECURITY THREAT?

The crossing of historical boundaries in a security and defence partnership between the US and India would create an enabling environment for several US weapons platforms to assemble part of their finished products in India. Lockheed Martin, for example, could assemble part of the aircraft F-21 in India and progress to the completion of the manufacture of the F-35. Facilities for the same were to be located in Turkey, until President Erdoğan installed the Russian S-400 missile defence system in Turkey instead.[18] In a move that reflects the narrow, siloed thinking of policymakers in India, a decision was taken to purchase five such systems and install them in India. The argument for such a move in the 1980s, or even presumably in the 1990s, had been the systems that were installed in India being insulated from data supplied to the PRC by Russia. The rationale behind this was the supposed distance between Russia and the PRC—they were openly hostile to each other in the 1980s and were not close during the post-Soviet era in the 1990s either. Only in the twenty-first century have Moscow and Beijing once again come closer not just tactically but also strategically.

In such a scenario, would this be the case with the S-400 as well? Of course, should the purchase of items from Russia to India not involve dollars but the rupee and the rouble, that would be an incentive to expand trade, especially in fields outside the purview of defence, such as resources. The relationship with Russia needs to be maintained, but with certain modifications. The Russians are indeed an outstanding people, as shown since the 1960s. This is in contrast to the US pressuring India, for instance, on the nuclear and space programme, although, this failed to hold back these programmes. Sanctions were applied on India, in a manner not seen at all in the case of China, and yet, these were overcome.

Given Moscow and Beijing's capabilities in using AI, and their cooperation in this field, it would be inadvisable to assume that because India was able to block snooping from Moscow through some of the war material purchased from that country in the 1980s or the 1990s, a similar result is certain now, when such systems are far more complex and the Sino-Russian bond much deeper. It is equally important to avoid signalling that India has tied itself to Russian platforms for at least a generation more, rather than factoring in the depth of the Sino-Russian alliance. Furthermore, we need to develop domestic alternatives and move to defence-related platforms from countries that are allied to partners and not foes of India as swiftly as possible. Such signalling would be poisonous for our relationship with Capitol Hill as well as with chancelleries across the world that are looking to ensure that India gets into shape in a way that it can deal with the threat from the PRC. The evolving contours of Russia–India cooperation must never be allowed to represent a considerable gift to the PRC, through actions that would make the establishment of a defence and security partnership between the US and India more difficult.

The relationship between New Delhi and Moscow has been entirely transactional rather than strategic from the Russian side from the start of the Yeltsin era. Among the most important of the benefits of the Sino-Russian alliance to the PLA is any collateral damage that might be suffered by the defence ties between India and the US as a consequence of Delhi's continuing heavy dependence on Russian platforms for its primary weapons systems. This includes the weapons that may be needed against kinetic action by the PLA on the Sino-Indian border. Given the absence of daylight between the military and security establishments of Beijing and Moscow, it is not improbable that the performance parameters and vulnerabilities of equipment sold to India by Russia may be made available to the PLA. Assurances to the contrary would almost certainly be anodyne rather than accurate, if the sentiment about past closeness is to be discounted.

HOSTING PRODUCTION AS A SECURITY MEASURE

It would be unsafe on the part of South Block to accept assurances from a power that has formed the closest of ties with a country that is no friend of India and has established a seamless working relationship with GHQ Rawalpindi over the decades, in their mutual quest to degrade the capabilities of India. This is a context where US weapons exporters are looking at India both as an assembly point and a market. Assembling part of their products in India would ensure that the price remains at par with competition offered by the Sino-Russian alliance in markets such as Southeast Asia and the Middle East. India would benefit from this not only through additional jobs but also from a greater number of weapons than what are needed domestically being produced within the country. This would partly, at least, defray the expenses of such acquisitions. Not just the US but the EU as well would look with favour on moving some of their production capacities to India as Berlin, London and Paris are now awakening to the security challenge posed by the Sino-Russian alliance in the era of Cold War 2.0.

In the past, aircrafts imported from Moscow were assembled in India but the more recent purchases have been off the shelf. Therefore, they have had a lesser impact on job totals in India, save for middlemen syndicates and the vast network of social media and conventional media boosters. This has led to the continued dependence of India on Russian defence supplies indefinitely into the future. India and Russia certainly need to boost their trade volumes but through increased imports of oil and gas by India rather than more weapons systems that are incompatible with platforms of India's western partners. Such a continuation would overlook the opportunity presented to

India of becoming an important part of the defence supply chain of the democracies and their allies across the world, including several that are close to India.

OVERCOMING THE FICTION OF NON-ALIGNMENT

Those who point to the incompatibility between a reliance on Russian weapons platforms and membership of structures designed to assist against the primacy of the Sino-Russian alliance in the Indo-Pacific, such as the Quadrilateral Security Dialogue (colloquially known as the Quad), are very quickly made the targets of social media and other attacks swarming around the general theme of 'selling out' to the US.[19] This is intended to divert attention from agents of the Sino-Russian alliance, who are on overdrive in India to prevent the coming together of the two biggest democracies in the world. They ceaselessly use both online as well as traditional media to fan suspicions in one country about the reliability and resilience of the other, thereby seeking to create a perception within the public in both the US and India that the other country would be an unwelcome and unreliable ally, when the contrary is true.

As mentioned earlier, it is as essential for the PRC to keep the US and India apart as it is for Washington to craft an effective partnership with India, now that Cold War 2.0 is increasing in its effects, both visible and silent. Russia needs to ensure that Washington and New Delhi remain separate, so that the nightmare of GHQ Rawalpindi, as well as the Sino-Russian alliance—an effective defence and security partnership between the US and India—never becomes a reality. The straitjacket of 'non-alignment' may be missing in explicit terms in the verbal and written outpourings coming from the recesses of the Lutyens Zone, but, in practice, this doctrine seems to very much be a concern in much policymaking. This needs to change, and quickly. Non-alignment was fiction even during Cold War 1.0, when exigencies caused a tilt towards Moscow. These days, circumstances are necessitating a tilt towards Washington, given that President Biden will give up his fantasies about Cold War 1.0 recurring. The White House needs to adopt policies towards India that are not as toxic as those pushed by President Clinton in the 1990s. They must involve a much closer engagement with India and an increase in the trust between the two sides.

5

Opportunity Knocks Twice at India's Door

Judging by its growth parameters in the four decades after Independence, India seems to have squandered the opportunities of the twentieth century generated by regaining its sovereignty. Once again, the China challenge confronting both the Atlantic as well as the Indo-Pacific powers has presented an opportunity in the twenty-first century that ought to be recognized and seized this time. Despite its achievements, among which is the continuance of its democracy and unity, India remains a democracy with much lower levels of transparency and accountability than the standard essential for the country to progress in a robust way. Beginning with flattering depictions of Nehru and continuing to the present, those in the media who write the first draft of history have overwhelmingly been swept up in tides of admiration for whoever is the leader of the day. Unless there is a systematic and factual assessment of the actual progress, or lack thereof, during each administration, the implementation of corrective mechanisms and the redressal of the situation caused by past errors would either be inadequate or absent.

PM Indira Gandhi placed the blame for the inflation created by her government's own policies on the global situation, saying that this was a problem faced by the entire world.[1] This may have been be so, but that conditions were the same or worse elsewhere ought not to have been used as an excuse for indifferent performance. It was on the glowing perception of his record as the chief minister of Gujarat that Indian voters placed their confidence in the party led by Modi in 2014. The belief that he was the better option for the future than his challenger, Rahul Gandhi, ensured a repeat victory in 2019. Sometimes, an individual is fortunate less in his choice of friends but more in the enemies that he has, and the BJP has been the beneficiary of a continuing lack of credibility at the leadership level of its principal challenger—the INC. However, beyond a point, the mood among voters is of 'any party other than the ruling party', and the principal factors behind that shift are usually dips in economic performance and personal security, no matter what part of the blame may reside in external factors.

DEMONETIZATION AND GST

The Indian economy was significantly disrupted by the manner in which the 2016 decision to demonetize the ₹1,000 note and change the design of the ₹500 notes was taken in a country where several lines of production have historically depended on printed currency to continue their operations. The existing currency was demonetized over a period of four hours.[2] The amount of currency that was exchanged for new legal notes by the banking system is known to be almost the entirety of the currency that was present in circulation at the time the decision was announced.[3] There are a few who claim without providing substantiation that the actual figures recycled back into the banking system are more than the total currency that was demonetized, which, they say, points to the likelihood of counterfeit currency being deposited for exchange as well, especially in bank branches that lacked the facility to speedily distinguish a counterfeit duplicate from legal currency.[4] Despite the immense dislocation caused to the economy by taking away as much as 86 per cent of its currency from circulation, the new ₹500 and ₹2,000 notes (when finally made available) did not seem to have any better defences against counterfeiting than the ones they replaced.

It bears mentioning that the US dollar is probably the most counterfeited currency in the world, yet it has never been demonetized.[5] This is to ensure its stability as a medium of reserves, both institutional and private, across the world. Demonetization is a nuclear option in the world of monetary policy, and the Reserve Bank of India (RBI) and the finance ministry should have ensured that liquidity was not affected by the changeover from old notes to new, since its effects, especially on small enterprises, could have been severe. The intention behind the shock demonetization was apparently to convert the economy of the country from a substantially currency-driven mechanism to a system that used near-zero levels of currency in its operations. This would indeed be desirable, but needed to be done over time by incentivizing the avoidance of currency in transactions by making such a method easy and advantageous to industry and commerce, especially smaller ones. Despite the manner in which the shock of demonetization was implemented, the use of printed currency returned as soon as its supply was adequate to meet its demand. A rigorous assessment of the costs and benefits of demonetization is awaited.[6]

PM Modi acted in good faith when he went ahead with the 2016 demonetization of 86 per cent of India's currency stock[7], as practically all his key advisors were lyrical about the presumed benefits of such a shock, and so, apparently, was the Governor of the RBI at the time[8]. Since the decision to demonetize had been made, it was incumbent on the Ministry of Finance and the RBI to ensure that economic activity did not suffer from a liquidity crisis in the way it did, which continued for a year before operations began to return to normalcy.[9]

Another significant economic decision was the introduction of the Goods and Services Tax (GST), which was a necessary reform implemented by PM Modi's government. As initially rolled out, the structure of the GST was complex enough to make compliance difficult for many.[10] Several wrinkles in the GST have been ironed out since, but many more remain, including a confusing array of rules and rates, many of which are very high. While chartered accountants (CAs) saw their custom increased by the GST when it was originally rolled out, several producers of goods and services found that much more time had to be dedicated to compliance than to ensuring that their businesses could face competition in the marketplace.

When the civil service continues with the colonial practice of designing laws and regulations without sufficient participation from elements of civil society, the policies that get implemented are usually suboptimal. This is especially true in a context where pride in the country, and appreciation of its past and confidence in its future, is often much lower within the policymaking community than verbal and written expressions suggest. It must be noted that the period after the onset of the Covid-19 pandemic has witnessed a flurry of reforms, several of which have aided the betterment of the economy. The Covid-19 pandemic substantially dislocated both the society as well as the economy in India, but it has also created opportunities through enterprises and investors from across the world, who have understood the consequences of the logic of Cold War 2.0.

INDIA: AN ALTERNATIVE TO THE PRC

The effects of the pandemic were multiplied by the PRC's responses, which often were in contrast to those seen during the earlier severe acute respiratory syndrome (SARS) pandemic, which affected not just China but the world a lot less severely. The multiplying restrictions and regulations brought into effect under General Secretary Xi have ensured that several enterprises from Taiwan, the US and Japan, in particular, are seeking relocation from the PRC.[11] Those running specialized enterprises in the PRC that produce dual use items (in the broad sense of that term) over the next few years are aware that markets across the world will place additional restrictions on admitting products made in China and, in a rising number of cases, block them altogether. This is among the reasons why the largest semiconductor chip manufacturer, Taiwan Semiconductor Manufacturing Company Limited (TSMC), has begun relocating its facilities to the US and its home base in Taiwan, and is also looking at India as a production centre.[12] Many problems in global supply chains were caused by the logistical challenges faced by external markets. These were a result of the measures taken to limit the spread of Covid-19 in China, and acted as a wake-up call to countries that have been heavily reliant on it for critical items in processing and manufacture, including India, as much of the intermediates in the domestic pharmaceutical industry come from China. This is driving the thrust towards getting access to more technologies and making the domestic market a bigger component of a company's success.

Enterprises in countries that have markets in the US and its allies, in particular, are looking at alternatives to production in China, a country that has changed dramatically since so many of them entered it with investments in the 1980s and 1990s. During this period, the PRC was a de facto ally of the US, even after the fall of the USSR in 1992. It was only during the twenty-first century that alarm bells were raised in key democracies about the way in which the PRC was on course to overtake the US as the most significant country in the world. Wages are much higher in the PRC, relative to the other options available, the PRC's oversight is multiplying, as is its transfer of technology, and the risk of peremptory action by the PRC authorities is real.[13] Small wonder that major brands are looking at Vietnam, India and other countries as sites for new plants, rather than further expanding their facilities in the PRC.

Although there is much public optimism about the attractions of India as an alternative to either relocating an existing plant or adding capacity, cautionary tales are multiplying. Some involve the incessant talk of 'deals' from policymakers when representatives of businesses meet them. Others recoil after seeing the expansive brand of bureaucratic discretion that still exists in a country that has consistently underperformed its potential. There are frequent newspaper headlines about 'single window clearances' and 'time-bound decision making', but, very often, such news does not get matched to actual experience. One of the reasons for this is the fact that blocking a project by creating hurdles in its implementation is very easy for elements so inclined in the bureaucracy, and more than a few businesspersons incentivize the officials they maintain in their group of friends to promote their interests by damaging those of a present or potential rival. The good news is that the second innings of PM Modi is proving to be much more successful in dismantling several such governmental blockages to growth and investment than was the case in the period between 2014 and 2019.[14]

Blocking a project carries much less risk of exposure and repercussions than fast-tracking a project. Acting in an expeditious manner is regarded as suspicious, even when the motivation is benign and the results obvious. In contrast, a leisurely approach to official decisions before a major or even, in many cases, a medium-scale project gets all the needed clearances is regarded as normal and, indeed, a mark of meticulousness. Just as there is a host of consequences prescribed (although usually not followed) for decisions that seem to have been taken for collateral reasons, there need to be consequences for those who are tardy in making decisions that impact the timeline for the expansion of income, jobs and output in a chosen location. The journey of relevant administrative files needs to be far more accessible online than it is now, especially to the intending investor. He or she should be able to track the progress of an award of the permissions needed to complete a project.

KICK-STARTING THE ECONOMY

That in India the entire country should eventually resemble a pristine forest is an admirable objective, but those placed in charge of giving or denying clearance to projects on environmental grounds should not forget that India has up to 13 million young citizens entering the job market every year. This is already a number beyond the level at which even the highest rates of growth in the past could meet, a factor which makes sustained double digit growth over the period of a generation the target that needs to be aimed for. Such government support for growth is visible in some cases—Modi 2.0 has performed much better than was expected on several parameters relating to the Covid-19 pandemic. For example, facilitating the development of vaccines in India. The same attention needs to be given to the manufacturing of drugs for effectively curing Covid-19.

This step is particularly noteworthy because the healthcare situation will be an important determinant of decisions about whether to invest in India or elsewhere, and, in this respect, healthcare, at least in select institutions, both public and private, must be of a quality that matches the best standards in the world. The medical profession in India has kept abreast of modern treatments and there has been an absence of impediments to their import. Of course, the much better course would be to ensure local production, as, together with food security, proper healthcare is a priority from the viewpoint of sufficiency in domestic production (although not necessarily solely through domestic players). What has been a cause of concern is that India has become dependent on the PRC in the requirements of its pharmaceutical industry at an accelerating pace over the last 15 years.[15] This has happened while China has, during this time, linked itself firmly to Pakistan and to some of the projects and objectives of the Pakistan military that are of concern to India. Self-sufficiency or speed in making decisions needs more than assurances from the leadership of India, a country where elections have often thrown up unexpected results.

Apart from self-sufficiency in the pharmaceutical industry, another necessary step to propel the economy would be a policy matrix reinforced by law that would provide an enabling environment for investment on the scale needed annually by India. India needs investments of around $200 billion from external sources in avenues that are unrelated to the hard currency flows of those who look to the financial arbitrage caused by high interest rates and a central bank policy favouring a falling rupee in the country.[16] The interests of such outside investors (a good proportion of whom may be round-tripping funds originating in India through transactions designed for the purpose of tax evasion) are often in conflict with those of the broader economy. Despite this, for decades, both the Ministry of Finance as well as the RBI gave such external interests a higher priority than domestic investors, a propensity first popularized by FM Singh between 1993 and 1996 and continued by his successors until FM Nirmala Sitharaman presented her first budget during Modi 2.0. What can be said about policy in a country like India, where external hard currency investment—in brick-and-mortar projects that create assets which cannot be removed from the country—has to navigate through far more difficult hoops than hard currency investors, who gain effortlessly from arbitrage caused by interest rate differences between their respective countries and India?

There is an urgent need for changes in laws and regulations that would make it more difficult for corrupt politicians and officials to harass and intimidate investors. GST and other building blocks in the system of direct and indirect taxation in India need to be genuinely simplified. The rates that are often designed not for future growth of a sector but for meeting the immediate (and constantly swelling) requirements of the government also need to be reduced. The effort at 'minimum government' needs to be revived to create an enabling investment for the substantial increases in domestic and external investment that the youth of the country need for their futures.

Australia has much fewer educational institutions than India and yet it has emerged as a major destination for overseas students. India has the capability, once the requisite policy framework is in place, to do much better in terms of the value added to the economy by an influx of overseas students into its educational institutions. In much the same way, health tourism, given the advances in the quality of healthcare in a multiplying number of institutions, could be another driver of growth in the economy, much more so than it already is.

CAPITALIZING ON CULTURAL HERITAGE

Tourism in general has lagged far behind its potential, partially because of the neglect of the heritage of India. The country has, since the days of colonialism, followed syllabi that showcase about a tenth of the overall history of India and make only passing references to the rest. Translations abound, and discoveries of ancient texts are still taking place. The history of India cannot be classified into periods that are based on religion, but need to be taken as a continuum that is the common heritage of every citizen, irrespective of their faith.

In the 1990s, *The Times of India* carried an op-ed piece on 'Indutva'. It covered a simple proposition that the cultural DNA of every Indian was a compound of the Vedic, Mughal and Western periods in the history of the land.[17] The three strands are intertwined and the resulting fusion (including significant aspects of lifestyle and culture) demonstrates that any theory that separates people of diverse faiths as being different in India is illogical. To give greater confidence to investors in our country, we need to develop social harmony and eliminate the efforts of people from across the political and broader societal spectrum to revive, in a variety of ways, the perception of the fundamental differences between the faiths in India. Countries where religious supremacy is practised are those where domestic achievements in various fields are low or absent. A moderate and modern society can best progress in the information age of the knowledge economy. It is India's good fortune that the overwhelming majority of its people, irrespective of faith or region, are moderate and are welcoming of modernity rather than seeking a return to medieval practices. This is the reason why eruptions of violence, especially between different communities, are still the exception rather than the rule in a country of 1.38 billion, of which no less than 230 million belong to minority faiths.

ADMINISTRATIVE REFORM AS THE WAY FORWARD

Administrative reform is the centrepiece of policies designed to create an enabling environment for massive flows of investment on an unprecedented scale. This has constantly been talked about, for instance in the Second Administrative Reforms Commission's report not to mention other commissions on administrative reform. Although a few of the suggestions made were followed up on, none of the comprehensive systems of reforms suggested in such reports were ever comprehensively implemented. When completed, reforms are usually partial, and, consequently, largely ineffective. An example is the induction of outside specialists into the administrative cadre system through special recruitment.[18] At least a third of the administrative services need to be populated with domain experts who have a demonstrable record of success in the achievement of objectives. The selections for such posts need to be made not based on the (often camouflaged) closeness to key politicians or officials but solely on the grounds of need and merit. The selection process must be transparent and accessible. Reform in India need not be a difficult process, provided there is political will and the absence of collateral considerations such as perpetuating vested interests.

There are many examples of the widespread disruption caused by small but motivated groups seeking to create chaos that, out of political calculation, are not checked in time. They are allowed to grow and finally reach levels that make their removal a process much more costly in terms of resources and manpower than would have been the case in the initial stages. For example, the IPS has several outstanding features to its credit, but these will only be effective if there is less political and bureaucratic micromanagement of the force's responses to particular situations. Just as a surgeon or an airline pilot needs to be left alone to complete his task, so should a police officer in all but a few exceptional situations. When the exception turns into the norm, the ecosystem needed for the promotion of investment gets affected. Capital gravitates to areas that are secure and untroubled by violence. Transfers get used to ensure the obedience of police personnel to the dictates of their political masters. This has been pointed out in some reports on police reforms, which, again, seem to have simply been pigeonholed for decades. Such a situation continued even after the Supreme Court of India, on 22 September 2006, mandated police reforms and gave directives that it deemed necessary, which, of course, were not carried out.[19]

ADOPTING A GROWTH MINDSET

It has often been said that a democracy cannot hope to replicate the success of an authoritarian state. The prosperity of an expanding list of democracies and the poverty of several authoritarian states show that this assumption is false. The PRC has, since the 1980s, been the exception that proves the rule that the best and certainly the most stable route to prosperity is genuine democracy. The onset of Cold War 1.0 provided an opportunity to the PRC that was discerned by Mao earlier, but it began to get actualized only during the 1970s, when the primary power on the other side of the Pacific Ocean was ready to accept such a tectonic shift in policy. Even earlier, it had been PM Pierre Trudeau of Canada who tore down the diplomatic walls that separated the PRC from North America, visiting the country and establishing friendly relations with several of its leaders. He was the pioneer who led the way for President Nixon to follow a few years later.

India has advantages that place it in the pole position to replicate the success of the PRC in the 1980s of becoming the most attractive destination for investment in the world. A policy and administrative matrix that is welcoming of innovation and enterprise would be linked to the natural advantages of the country, which is its abundance of manpower and its internal market. Whatever be its initial shortfalls and deficiencies, the adoption of GST has brought closer the day when one nation will have one market. Similarly, trade needs to be encouraged across the globe, with domestically manufactured products seeking markets worldwide. Both the central as well as state governments already have control over vast areas of land, part of which could be turned over for the creation of industrial, commercial, software and business parks with attendant facilities. An enabling environment for quality healthcare, housing and education would complete the range of reasons why India could become the 'must go' destination for investors, which the PRC had been transformed to in the 1980s by the genius of Paramount Leader Deng.

Despite these advantages and possibilities, India remains a country where its elites (including the intelligentsia) indulge in self-doubt about its capability to break out into the double-digit growth trajectory that is needed over a generation to enable the people to secure the lifestyles that they merit through their innate capacities. An obsessive fear of failure has often caused both politicians and bureaucrats to avoid the unfamiliar and to remain embedded in policy furrows that have long passed their expiry date.

Those who gingerly seek to map out new terrain often scurry back to past practices, often after making changes that are more cosmetic than real. In actuality, the potential of the country that is the world's largest democracy is immense, and the major constraint has long been a policy matrix that is unsuited to evolving conditions, much as a dress that was a good fit when a person was young would no longer be suitable some years later and would be increasingly awkward to wear. Policies in India get formed in a manner that resists change, whereas they need, in the twenty-first century, to be like prefabricated structures, easily capable of removal, refitment and expansion. While a 'single window' is indeed desirable for the promotion of investment, what is needed is an open door—of course, with discreet surveillance systems in place and monitoring mechanisms that ensure the discovery and removal of the few problem cases that may arise. Blocking 99 proposals in an effort to catch a sole rat in the pack makes much less sense than admitting hundred proposals and swiftly discovering the rat based on the empowerment of the 99, which will strengthen us.

ALIGNMENT AND AFFILIATION

It is essential to clearly signal that India has chosen its side now that Cold War 2.0 has begun. There must be no ambiguity about this, and the choice needs to be conveyed not necessarily in words but through deeds, which can include:

- the formalization, in operational terms, of the Quadrilateral Alliance, based on the Quad, which includes Australia, India, Japan and the US;
- the setting up of Quad bases in each of the four member countries;
- the signing of an Indo-Pacific charter between like-minded powers that seek to protect freedom of navigation and absence of hegemony in the Indo-Pacific;
- the Quad powers need to initiate closer ties with Indonesia, for its unique capabilities and characteristics, and Vietnam, for its indomitable spirit.

Over the decades, since colonialism began to fade away from the shores of Asia, Vietnam has stood out as a beacon of defiance against outside authority that expresses, in full measure, the sentiment of the coalition of the willing that has formed to ensure free and easy access in the waters of the Indo-Pacific and to protect the independence and sovereign rights of the countries in the region.

As for the US, there has been apprehension within elements of the policymaking matrix in New Delhi that President Biden will differ from President Trump in his approach towards India, Pakistan and China. That Biden has, in his previous avatars, not found the time or the opportunity to visit India has been noticed, so have the multiple times he has visited

China and Pakistan. Biden has advanced his political career by conforming to the perceived political needs of the day. The situation in the context of the US and India and Pakistan and China is very different now than it was in the 1980s or the 1990s, which should get factored into the policy formulation in the White House, as well as to the National Security Council and the Department of State. Policies in stable democracies are shaped less by personalities than by events and interests, and the strategic tailwind is now in India's favour in a manner that was absent earlier.

Virtual conversations cannot compensate for the lost advantages of physical meetings. Whatever be the security barriers to prevent the leakage of conversations, there is the lurking realization that any such conversation can be, and most probably, will be, recorded. Conversations done while, say, taking a walk in the garden could ensure that much more of the actual motivations or apprehensions of those engaged in such discussions get revealed. The consequences of not being able to gauge the true motivations and affiliations of foreign nations can be great. For example, the 1962 experience of India being left to fend for itself during the conflict with China left Nehru surprised. That ought not to have been the case. Those in the 'non-aligned' movement, who Nehru believed could be counted on for support, behaved in the way one would expect those who are 'non-aligned' to behave—in a non-committal manner. Keeping aside the collateral effects of this action (such as the US ramping up its assistance of Pakistan), whatever benefits India secured as a consequence of the Nehruvian policy of non-alignment were actually gained as a result of the country no longer remaining non-aligned in any meaningful sense of the term. The policy followed by the South Block was aligned with the USSR in all but name, beginning with Nehru, becoming more pronounced with Indira Gandhi, further deepening during the anti-India administration of President Nixon.

The external marks of alignment may have differed—the fig leaf displayed by India was that it was not a member of any pact formed by the USSR, nor did Soviet troops use India as a base for any of their operations, such as those conducted in Afghanistan. However, the tone adopted by Nehru during the Suez crisis caused by Israel, the UK and France in 1956 and the invasion of Hungary the same year by the USSR were demonstrably not the same. The reticence in joining the global condemnation, by democracies, of the USSR during, for example, the crushing of dissent in Czechoslovakia in 1968 was accompanied by repeated denunciations of the US policy in Vietnam. The war ended badly for Washington, but not before several of the countries that are now in the ASEAN had gained from the supply of material for the prosecution of the war against the unification of the country by Ho Chi Minh.

Beginning with Harry Truman's period in office and continuing under Dwight Eisenhower, the US identified, as its own interests, the Asian countries that had been colonized by European powers. This was in contrast to the approach of President Roosevelt, who understood and expressed the need for the European powers to accept that the principles listed in the Atlantic Charter applied not just to Europeans but to Asians and Africans as well. There was no dilution of non-alignment in the opposition of Nehru to the Suez misadventure of the three invading powers or to the manner in which Vietnam (together with Cambodia and Laos) was carpet bombed by the United States Air Force (USAF) and in the way in which South Vietnam was sought to be occupied by 600,000 US troops and counting. Each such soldier had the effect of a recruitment poster for the Viet Cong and the North Vietnam Army. Similar candour was lacking in the matter of the USSR's actions.

Non-alignment should not mean silence and tacit acceptance of policies of either superpower that need to be opposed. A similar candour as was adopted in the case of Suez or Vietnam ought to have been shown in the case of the USSR's transgressions of the freedom of nominally independent countries. For example, the events in Hungary and Czechoslovakia. That India was, in practice, non-aligned during Cold War 1.0 is a myth that continues to be recycled and apparently accepted as the truth by much of the foreign policy community in India. The reality was that New Delhi was, in effect, aligned with the USSR during almost the entirety of Cold War 1.0, just as the PRC was aligned with the US during the latter half of that period.

CHOOSING A GLORIOUS PRESENT

Returning to the theme of interpersonal relationships between those paired not only at the summit level but lower down as well, such relationships could create trust in the discretion and intent of the one person towards the other (and, in some cases, vice-versa). In that case, the views expressed will be devoid of spin and camouflage, and represent an accurate rather than a deliberately slanted portrayal of the other person's views. Were PM Modi to establish such a relationship between himself and some of the leaders of ASEAN in a manner that was absent in his relationship with CCP General Secretary Xi, they may be more candid in expressing their fears about China than they have been in public. The reality is that the leaders of ASEAN are well aware of the PRC's drive, through diplomacy or the PLA, to expand its influence in the region such that a 'Jimi' relationship gets forged with more ASEAN member states, similar to what has already happened in the case of Laos and Cambodia. As mentioned earlier, a Jimi relationship is a Tang dynasty concept that stresses the importance of giving outward respect to the independence and sovereign rights of another power while ensuring that it marches to the tune of Beijing. Although this would not get expressed in public, or even in official conversations, some of the most consequential members of the ASEAN would look with approval at a de facto formalization of the Quadrilateral Security Dialogue as a security construct and, once such a development takes place, would join (gingerly at first but more emphatically with time) in some of the operations of the Quad.[20]

While the US has, since President Obama's term, joined Tokyo in welcoming greater depth in the partnership of the Quad, Australia was hesitant at first, due to its extensive trade with the PRC. However, this has changed, and the former Australian PM Scott Morrison has been forthright in standing up to the tactics of Beijing to awe him into at least partial submission. He has, for example, strengthened the Quad, signed a free trade agreement with India, but not with China, and called for an open and transparent investigation into the origins of Covid-19, angering Beijing.[21]

That leaves India, which, in several respects (at least to those outside the portals of South Block), continues with its see-saw policy of hugging the President of Russia and promoting his interests one week, and, in the next, repeating that charming cameo with the President of the US. It may be remembered that India was practically the only country in the world to welcome even the short-lived coup in August 1991 against CPSU General Secretary Gorbachev, when the regime had already entered its death throes.[22] Now, India appears to be the only major country in the world that operationally seems to have refused to accept that Russia is very different from its predecessor, the USSR, or that Moscow has been locked into a close twenty-first century defence and security alliance with Beijing that has only increased in intensity since Xi became the CCP general secretary in 2012. Will such a situation remain, or will New Delhi accept the reality in the manner that Canberra, under its present government, has? That there is still doubt about the need for this, even after the 15 June 2020 clash at Galwan, indicates that, in India, outdated policies linger for what seems like eternity.

India's policies towards health, education or the economy, and not just defence, must be formulated with reference to the challenges faced by the country as well as the opportunity provided by the Cold War 2.0. This is the chance of a generation growing up during the tenure of an individual of proven good fortune—Narendra Modi. More and more of those at the lower levels of policymaking appear to be smelling the coffee and getting the message about the imperative of changing policies to take advantage of the opportunities created by a paradigm shift. Indications are that such clarity has been percolating to the higher levels as well. Ultimately, whether Modi does for India what Deng did for China will depend on him. The window of opportunity created by Cold War 2.0 may be closed, especially by policy missteps, as has happened in the past. India is a country with a glorious past and a glorious future but, thus far, never a glorious present. The DNA strand of foreign policy must intertwine with domestic policy to ensure that the country escapes from the high-potential, low-performance trap that it was stuck in during the previous century.

6

India's 'Near Abroad'

In Russia, the term 'near abroad' has been used to describe the 14 republics that broke away from the USSR during its final days. A better description would be to describe a country's near abroad as those countries that are close to it strategically or ought to be—nations that need to be brought closer in their relationships. It must be added that the term should apply both ways. Thus, each of the countries designated as India's near abroad should reciprocally have India as part of their own 'near abroad'.

Countries become neighbours by the accident of history. In contrast, the list of states that form a part of a wider redefinition of the near abroad of a particular country get chosen for the synergy that they bring, should the relationship between the two sides move into the stage of a stronger partnership. Since Nehru's period in office, India has tacitly used the term near abroad in a Russian sense, which is to refer to its South Asian neighbours, whereas what counts is less geographical and more about national self-interest. Southeast and East Asia have long been of much greater significance to Indian interests than some of the states of South Asia, which have nevertheless occupied the centre stage in policymaking.

Some are given attention not because of any benefits they bring but because of the problems they create. This has intermittently been true of some South Asian countries. However, it is especially true of Pakistan, whose dominant influence—the military—has, from the start of its existence, seen India as an enemy that needs to be weakened and finally, split into fragments. Especially since the closing years of the 1990s, GHQ Rawalpindi and the Central Military Commission in Beijing have coordinated their strategies and actions. They have been designed to degrade the state of readiness of India's defences. Such cooperation with a self-acknowledged enemy of India crossed a red line early in the tenure of General Secretary Xi who has, since the beginning of his tenure in 2012, signed on to the PLA strategy of using the asymmetric skills developed by the PLA and GHQ Rawalpindi to box India in, as seen in Kashmir and the Northeast, thereby shrinking its capabilities of emerging as the third superpower after the US and the PRC.

CHINA-PAKISTAN VS INDIA-AMERICA

It was not rocket science for the CCP leadership core to understand that there was a limit beyond which the overall relationship with India would get adversely affected by the expansion of the India-specific collaboration of the PLA with GHQ Rawalpindi. Nonetheless, the confidence within Beijing of the dysfunctionality and the malleability of decision-making in India was so great that, years ago, a level of cooperation between GHQ Rawalpindi and the PLA was reached that was no longer tolerable to India. The surplus of exports from China to India has increased in tandem with the joint efforts of PLA and GHQ Rawalpindi to damage the security interests of India—a country that seems on track to generate $100 billion as annual surplus for the PRC, which is more than sufficient to fund its numerous initiatives against New Delhi.[1] The persisting prevalence of decision-making silos in the Lutyens Zone has engendered confidence in Beijing that greater pressure affecting the particular silo dealing with border management and defence would not have an effect on the policy silos dealing with cooperation between New Delhi and Beijing in international fora or those handling commerce.

The two objectives of economic and military dominance were put on a fast track and became the primary subject of PRC diplomacy with India. However, the question of resolving the border issue was given such a low a priority by Beijing that nearly two dozen interactions between the special representatives of the two sides on the border issue have, thus far, not led to substantive results. Such a lack of progress suited the interests of GHQ Rawalpindi as well as the strategies of the PLA where shifting the dotted-line border with India was concerned. As predicted by planners in Beijing, the resulting stalemate made no difference to the volume of trade between the PRC and India. During the tenure of the National Democratic Alliance (NDA) government, which was formed on 26 May 2014, the balance of trade moved against India, although the situation is different in 2022, and the reliance on PRC platforms for a range of products has intensified to levels that constituted a threat to the national interest even during the United Progressive Alliance (UPA) period. In particular, metadata from India has flowed in copious quantities to the PRC and are assisting in improving its AI capabilities, not just in the commercial but also in the military sphere. In such a context, the ban on several Chinese mobile applications announced by PM Modi's government has been a welcome change from the laissez-faire approach of previous administrations to such a danger.[2]

In effect, data from India is proving to be an important force multiplier for the PLA and a means for the PRC to fund its rising financial commitment to Pakistan. Data enables Chinese companies to bid at prices just above those of its competitors for acquiring assets or just below to find customers. Several business houses and businesspeople have become reliant on the profits made from destroying domestic production through importing substitutes from the PRC, which have deliberately been maintained at attractively low prices. As was pointed out much earlier in an article in the *Far Eastern Economic Review*, in China, the price of inputs is set by the price needed to compete against external rivals in overseas markets.[3] A further sweetener has been the extension of loans to several such entities and individuals from PRC-controlled financial institutions—a dependence that has made them either closeted or open promoters of the interests of the PRC, even when they go not only against the interests of India but also against their own interests, such as permitting uniformed personnel in locations that are legally part of India or by taking over ports or other facilities there. PoK is an example of the first and the takeover of Hambantota port in Sri Lanka of the second.

The silver lining is that the dense network of relationships that has been expensively and meticulously cultivated in the US by Beijing proved of little value in preventing several of the decisions of the China-related Trump administration, including the expansion in defence and security cooperation with Taiwan. Recent trends have strengthened the view that such PRC-backed networks in the US would regain their old potency during Biden's term.

Not that President Trump was able to make a substantial difference in the eventually self-destructive dependence of the

US corporates on the PRC for much of their manufactures and other supplies. This has created a powerful lobby in the US (as in India) that has been opposed to any policy that accepts the reality of Cold War 2.0, seeking to ignore that situation and return to the days of presidents from Carter to Clinton, and, to a lesser extent, Bush and Obama. During all those years, the US remained the most effective force multiplier for Chinese technology and the expansion of its Comprehensive National Power (CNP). Despite the Europeanist background of President Biden, Secretary of State Anthony Blinken and National Security Advisor Jake Sullivan, President Biden has himself made a few wise choices of individuals, such as US Trade Representative Katherine Tai, who understand the danger posed by the PRC to democracies. Hence, the jury is still out on whether he is accepting the reality of Cold War 2.0 (PRC–US) or seeking to continue the policies adopted during Cold War 1.0 (USSR–US) during his term in the White House.

A country working hard to poison the US–India relationship is Russia. While in India, interlocutors from Russia stress their (naturally private) distaste for Beijing, in the US, the PRC interlocutors with the US are often dismissive about the extent and intent of the relationship between Russia and PRC in the Xi–Putin era.[4] Both say what they wish their interlocutors to hear and believe, not the factual truth. Of course, the covert reality is that both Moscow and Beijing (and in the latter's calculations, where India is concerned) Islamabad as well, are working together to ensure the actualization of the many common results they seek to create, including widening any existing distance between US and Indian policymakers in key aspects such as defence and security. Both Moscow and Beijing are increasingly shedding any camouflage of their common desire to ensure a steady rise in the extent of public support for the Left and Right fringe in the US at the cost of the mainstream middle, an objective shared by Islamabad and Beijing for India. This is apparent from outpourings of Russian television or CGTN. AI is being used to manipulate messaging on social media so as to accelerate the polarization of the American and Indian societies, which is harming the stability and harmony needed for an atmosphere that is conducive to excellence in the knowledge economy.[5]

BREAKING FREE OF SINO-RUSSIAN DEPENDENCE

India is not the only country of appreciable size that has become a milch cow for the securing metadata for the development of China's AI capabilities. The US is another example, and here, efforts by the Trump administration to replicate PM Modi's moves in India of banning some of the important mobile applications sucking data out and transferring them back to entities serving the PRC have been stymied by courts that have ignored the reality of Cold War 2.0 and its security imperatives. The US has been in a state of an existential war of systems with the PRC for some time, but several of the institutions in that democracy have yet to accept that fact and grasp its implications in the comprehensive manner that the other side has.

There is an immediate link between the metadata transmitted through apps and other social media accessories, such as cell phones, and the military capabilities of a sophisticated power. In this context, the CCP leadership core has been wise to ban such apps within the country, except those that are home-grown and fully under its control. There is no separation in an authoritarian State between private and public, as both are equally controlled by the State and are expected to carry out its commands and accept its priorities as their own. That this is the situation in China has hardly been a secret, which is why it was somewhat of a surprise that the national security apparatus in India seemed to be unconcerned about the manner in which cell phone brands from companies with internationally known PLA linkages have established a position of dominance in the Indian market.[6]

Bureaucratic hurdles (often caused by moves to sabotage domestic competitors) have prevented the development of substitutes designed and produced within India, and it is extraordinary how many Indian start-ups with the potential of challenging foreign competitors have been derailed through regulatory and other hurdles. This is clearly a systematic use of the governance machinery to ensure India's dependence on foreign (particularly PRC and Russian) technology, including in defence. PM Modi's call for greater self-reliance in such fields is welcome and needs to be activated down the line rather than remaining a pious hope in practice. For almost two decades, the PRC has substantially increased its metadata penetration in India, while India's dependence on Russia for core defence deals and the flow of money to both continue unabated. This is happening despite apparent efforts by PM Modi to reverse this course and ensure that the PRC is not given the financial surpluses needed to empower the Pakistan military as well as the PLA.

It is difficult to understand how India expects to attract a significant share of the production units initiating their relocation from the PRC if it is less than energetic in ensuring that its own dependence on China in key sectors gets scaled down. Doing so would protect India from funding and assisting the capabilities of the GHQ Rawalpindi–PLA defence and security alliance against it. Furthermore, it would demonstrate to the international community, and particularly investors, the side that India has chosen in Cold War 2.0. This needs to be done in a manner shorn of the ifs and buts that have long characterized much of policy in India.

CONNECTING WITH INDIA'S NEAR ABROAD: INDONESIA

A recital of the near abroad of India (not forgetting the fact that India, too, forms part of the near abroad of these countries) needs to begin with Indonesia and Iran. There needs to be a simultaneous push towards much closer relations with both the nations. Indonesia has the largest number of Muslims in the world and India the third highest.[7] Unlike the situation in Pakistan, the country with the second-largest Muslim population on the planet, Wahhabism has been kept at bay in Indonesia. In overwhelming number, the Muslims of Indonesia are similar to the Muslims of India in being moderate and open to modern influences. It needs to be kept in mind that the Quran enjoins believers to constantly learn from experience gained through the march of time. This is the opposite of the effort of those who may be called the Wahhabi International to fossilize habits of thought and action. What replaces them is a catechism filled with ritual and a thought matrix that promotes contempt and hatred for an expansively described Other. Only by keeping away individuals from thought independent of the nostrums peddled by Wahhabi preachers can the latter be certain that their flock will not understand and operationalize the need to move into modes of thought and action that are congruent with harmony and success in the twenty-first century.

In both Indonesia as well as in India, Muslims have taken to modern education in large numbers, especially Muslim women. Ensuring that the curricula taught in schools reflects the need for skills with present-day relevance is imperative if the spectre of large-scale youth unemployment is to be rolled back and eliminated. Ensuring that women are respected in the manner enjoined in the Quran rather than treated as less than men is equally vital, because such respect for women within a household promotes the social values needed in a stable and prospering community. For more than three decades, mainstream society in Indonesia has been engaged in a battle against the hard-line fringe of its majority faith, a battle where such fringe elements seem to be making progress, although less than in the neighbouring Malaysia.

India and Indonesia need to ensure a system of visa-free entry, with a proviso that 72 hours before boarding the ship, aircraft and, hopefully soon, train that can take them to the other country, details about the intending visitor should be submitted online. Each individual needs to undergo online checks, and the few who are suspected of being a part of the fringe rather than the mainstream of theological thought need to be flagged either for refusal of entry (communicated in advance) or be monitored on arrival to ensure that the purposes of the visit are benign. Reciprocally, there are several locations in India that would be of immense interest to Muslims worldwide, such as Ajmer Sharif, and these need much more publicity than has been given to them in the past. Sites of importance to the Buddhist, Muslim and Hindu heritage in India need to be brought back to their earlier state, so that they become the focus for groups of visitors, ideally of all faiths. A house of worship is a house of worship for all human beings, although the discretion as to whether to admit all or restrict entry to a narrower band needs to be left to the concerned religious structure. It is not the business of the state to micromanage such matters, save in the case of structures that have been renovated at State expense. To ensure that these sites are presentable and attractive for international tourists, renovations could be opened to those interested in doing so, such as what has taken place at Bodh Gaya and Shravasti in the case of Buddhists. If the path taken by Lord Ram from Ayodhya to Sri Lanka were to be reconstructed, it would become the focus of attention, as well as admiration and devotion, across the globe. A rediscovery of India's past is essential in reclaiming the future from the despondency of much of the previous centuries. Moreover, Indonesia needs to do the same. There may be more than a few Borobudurs awaiting discovery in remote corners of this fascinating country. Efforts at uncovering the heritage of the past ought not to be concentrated in Bali but in the country as a whole.

In a world where barriers have been erased through technology, a syncretic approach to society and culture needs to be made the norm. Religious supremacy is as odious an ideology as racial supremacy. Whether it be India or Indonesia, or indeed Iran, the entire history of these countries needs to be exposed to the people and celebrated. Just as culture in India is a fusion of the Vedic, Mughal and western streams, so is culture in Indonesia and Iran a fusion of multiple historical periods. There have been efforts by bigots to seek an exclusivist interpretation of history (or what is regarded as the only significant part of it, which, in the British colonial era, in India was only the part beginning with the entry of the British into the country). The farther back in Indian history from the colonial period that actual events and episodes were, the lesser was the attention paid to them, with large segments of the historical record being dismissed as myths. Nehru spoke of the 'Discovery of India.' What India needs to do is rediscover itself, as do Indonesia and Iran. The bilateral relationship between Indonesia and India, and between India and Iran will be crucial in influencing the geopolitics of the future, especially in the Indo-Pacific.

ANOTHER NEAR ABROAD: IRAN

Iran is regarded as the most important cultural influence on the Shia population of the world. Since the takeover of government by followers of Ayatollah Khomeini in 1979, the country has had a governance system in which the Shia clergy play a key role. The difficulty is that the Khomeinist doctrine, in many respects, does not fit perfectly with traditional Shia beliefs. The Khomeinist doctrine is closer to Wahhabism in its characterization of the Other and in the strident nature of its opposition to regimes with which Tehran has a fundamental difference of Weltanschauung. It is expansionist and missionary in its nature, much like the Wahhabi; it appears to have been accepted as an article of faith by the theologians who wrested control of Iran from the Pahlavi dynasty that a focus on the issue of Palestine would lead to a rapid expansion in the number of followers of the version of the faith practised in Iran. If not that, it would, at least, make huge swathes of the population support a friendly relationship with Tehran. This has not happened but, like with several other authoritarian structures, the Khomeinists in Iran have refused the empirical evidence of the indifferent results of their focus on Palestine, even in the Arab world. That the Arab world regards the Palestinian cause as critical in their moods and decisions has been less than true from the start, and this is visibly the case now.

Under the Trump administration, the attention given to the Palestine issue has mostly been of a variety that promotes the interests of Israel, a course of action that has proved wrong numerous 'experts on the Middle East' who had forecast hellfire in the strategic moves on this issue, such as the shift of the US embassy from Tel Aviv to Jerusalem in 2018. Some of the declared followers of Trump may be wholly repulsive, such as those who believe in the legitimacy of Hitler and his party's belief system. It would, however, be inaccurate to argue that Trump is himself an anti-Semite. Tehran's fixation on the Palestinian cause ignores or underplays Israel's influence on events along with its all-weather ally—the US—and causes headwinds for Iran that have blocked the country from the development that its gifted population has the potential for. Iran under its Khomeinist system of governance represents another example of the manner in which policymakers and the self-defeating (where 'self' refers to the country) matrix of policies that they conjure up constrain the progress of a country far more effectively than the impact of hostile powers.

In this context, the Joint Comprehensive Plan of Action (JCPOA) that was backed by President Obama and signed in 2015 was a significant breakthrough not only in constraining and more effectively monitoring Iran's nuclear-related progress but in assisting reformists within the country to seriously dilute many of the pernicious effects of the Khomeinist system, especially on the freedom of Iranian citizens. Its implementation would have successfully augmented the influence of reformists over hardliners in the Iranian establishment. President Trump's withdrawal from the agreement in 2018 has, in fact, been a strategic setback for the US and a gain for the Sino-Russian alliance, exactly similar to Trump's withdrawal from the Trans-Pacific Partnership (TPP) just three days after shifting his residence to the White House in 2017.

This course of action was adopted because, from the very first month of his presidential term, Trump was obsessed with getting re-elected in 2020, and hence, on implementing policies that he believed would ensure a second term. Much of the volubility regarding the 'China threat' was less a consequence of understanding the logic of Cold War 2.0 than it was a reaction to the fact that public opinion in the US (to the dismay of the Atlanticists who focus on Russia as the threat and present the PRC as an opportunity) was becoming increasingly hostile to the PRC. Apart from 'dog-whistle' racism, stoked by some supporters of Trump and cheered on by him, what helped build Trump's impressive vote tally on 3 November 2020 was several voters' belief that Biden was soft on China, or, at least, much softer than Trump had been and would be if given a second term. Such a view does not reflect the reality, but it must be remembered that perception rather than actuality drives voter behaviour.

Overall, the social fabric of the US was severely damaged due to the tendency of the Trump White House to openly encourage behaviours that had been reducing since the 1960s. These behaviours were allowed to resurface through the vicious campaign launched by a section of the Republican Party on President Obama—the first African-American to be sworn in as president of the US. The attacks on President Obama continued throughout his term and created an enabling environment for the racist impulses that motivated events, such as the storming of the Capitol by mobs on 6 January 2021, in an effort to use extra-constitutional and violent means to prevent the process of ratifying the election of Joe Biden as the next president of the US from moving ahead. A similar reckless disregard for consequences suffused some of the other actions of President Trump, including the US administration's withdrawal from the JCPOA with Iran. President Trump's national security advisor, John Bolton, was lobbying for such a move from within the administration after he was appointed to the post in 2018 and, within months, successfully carried out the withdrawal.

Bolton's publicly available written and spoken words clarify that he favoured an all out military conflict between the US and Iran to try and take out that country's nuclear and missile programme. Fortunately, aware that the US public was averse to waging overseas wars, this was too much of an ask even for President Trump to accede to. Earlier, in 2003, 'take an action and let the chips fall where they may' was the implicit credo adopted by President Bush when he invaded Iraq, a policy that derailed the counterterrorism process in Afghanistan, which ultimately ended up strengthening the diplomatic footprint of Tehran in an unprecedented manner in Baghdad, just as Trump's withdrawal from the TPP in 2017 opened the door for the PRC to initiate moves for a Regional Comprehensive Economic Partnership (RCEP), with Beijing at its core. It was formally agreed to on 15 November 2020. While India kept away, two members of the Quad—Australia and Japan—signed it, a decision that both are likely to regret later, along with the ASEAN countries.

The logic of Cold War 2.0 is constraining trade opportunities for items produced in the PRC. As the dynamics of this situation pan out across the globe, trading partners will not accept Beijing's concessions to Canberra and Tokyo in the RCEP negotiations. As part of these concessions, Australia and Japan can have their produce welcomed by China, a country that will find its options becoming constricted by the logic of events.

In the Trump administration, despite the presence of members, like John Bolton, who had unreal expectations of the US potential, the White House, the Pentagon and the state department understood the need to have some degree of cordiality with India, which has been a necessary partner of the US despite maintaining links with Tehran. Such a 'bridging' role is a natural fit for India, which is presumably why the Chabahar Port project was kept out of the sanctions net by the US, even under Trump.[8] Unfortunately, India's purchases of petrochemical products from Iran was not left out of the ambit of the US sanctions, and the sale of such items by Iran to India very quickly began to dwindle, only to stop altogether once the period of sanctions waiver ended.[9] It ought not to have been beyond the competence of the finance ministry and the RBI to devise ways of getting the oil, possibly through barter or by trading in rupees. To be accepted as a reliable partner by Tehran, it was necessary for New Delhi to continue its purchases of Iranian oil, and the stoppage of such trade caused a trust deficit between the two capitals that worked to the advantage of Beijing and Moscow, while harming the interests of India.

The officials in the South Block decided to challenge the White House not in what was the desirable course for continuing with purchasing Iranian oil, but by placing orders for installing the Russian S-400 missile defence system on Indian territory. This was to guard against the PRC, a country that was the closest military partner of Russia, and which had installed the S-400 and presumably had been made aware of its vulnerabilities. The other country that the system was intended to guard was Pakistan, whose military has long been close to the PLA, and which presumably would have been assisted by that force to tackle any situation created by the installation of the S-400 system in India. Both Beijing and Moscow regarded India's purchase of the S-400 as the secret weapon that would stop the development of a military-to-military partnership between Washington and New Delhi in its tracks, to the level that would fatally threaten an attempted invasion by the PRC into Indian territory, which could be carried out in synchronization with GHQ Rawalpindi. Wiser counsel in Washington has ensured that this has not happened, despite efforts of anti-India lobbies to get the US administration to impose the Countering America's Adversaries Through Sanctions Act (CAATSA) sanctions based on operationalizing the S-400 deal. Consequently, the opportunity to establish strong ties with Iran was missed.

DECISIONS AND CONSEQUENCES IN WEST ASIA

It remains to be seen how the Modi government will navigate its way out of the consequences of the problems caused by past decisions that had the effect of distancing New Delhi and Washington, despite growing strategic congruence. A partnership with the US is needed to ensure security for everyone in the Indo-Pacific, to develop a more robust deterrent to the PLA's activism and to stop further aggression on the Sino-Indian border than would be the case were New Delhi to confront this threat without the close involvement of Washington in matters of supply and provision of intelligence. Next, the necessary relationship with Iran must be continued as a demonstration of 'strategic independence'—something that needs to be demonstrated through actions rather than words. The relationship with Iran needs to be rebuilt, given that Tehran would be aware of the fact that GHQ Rawalpindi is an accessory to covert moves to cause mayhem in Iran through groups embracing violence as an instrument of coercion; or the plight of the Shia population in Pakistan, in contrast to the Shia community in India.

That India needs to continue expanding and deepening

its ties with the GCC and to powers such as Japan, France, the UK and Germany is a given. France, in particular, has consistently backed India; so has Israel. Within the GCC, the advent of Mohammed bin Salman Al Saud, colloquially known as MBS, as the leader of the Kingdom of Saudi Arabia indicates a change, at long last, in its traditional policy of boosting the capabilities of the Wahhabi International. MBS is, of course, no liberal democrat; he is a votary of the absolutist principle of monarchy that has served (together with Wahhabism) as the basis of the rule of the Al Sauds over the country named after them. However, by openly rejecting Wahhabism and in seeking to dilute the influence of adherents of the creed in Saudi Arabia, MBS has shown prescience and leadership, and needs to be encouraged rather than getting pilloried by those who want instant change in Saudi Arabia.[10] If he was made to step down, it would lead to the full authority of the Wahhabis returning, rather than any tilt towards liberal or, indeed, any other kind of democracy. It would be a step back.

In countries like Egypt, the 2011 Arab Spring was followed soon afterwards by a Wahhabi winter, and this needs to be avoided in a country that has the custody of Medina and Mecca. Closer ties between India and Saudi Arabia would be helpful in battling the turbulence created by terror groups that embrace one or the other forms of Wahhabism. As yet, those groups that have adopted the Khomeinist doctrine have left India unmolested, and this is another essential by-product of good relations with Tehran.

TAPPING INTO AFRICA'S POTENTIAL

The African continent is vast and India's resources and diplomatic bandwidth is limited. Consequently, there needs to be a short list of African countries that ought to be prioritized. These are Kenya and South Africa on the mainland of the continent, and the Republic of Madagascar in the Indo-Pacific. Like India, both Kenya and South Africa are part of the Commonwealth and an increasing part of their populations speak English—the international link language. Although Churchill confined his version of the English-speaking world (or the Anglosphere) to countries such as Canada, New Zealand and Australia, besides the US, India has almost as many citizens who understand and can converse in English as the US, and will, before long, overtake the US in the number of English speakers in the country.

The twenty-first century Anglosphere, which includes both India and these African nations, must be based not on the blood of the body (or, in other words, race) but on the blood of the mind. The mind rather than the physical body is what separates human beings from other species. In such a construct, India can play a prominent role, given that the English language is understood across most parts of India, and is gaining popularity, even in states such as Bihar and Uttar Pradesh. The twenty-first century Anglosphere could emerge as a diplomatic and soft power force multiplier for India were policymakers to take advantage of this factor rather than ignore it, as was done by Nehru, who apparently regarded English as a language meant only for the elite, such as himself. Only in the recent past have some far-sighted state governments ensured that the language becomes accessible to the underprivileged through the public schooling system—a trend that needs to be encouraged rather than held back.

United by the English language, India could focus on Kenya and South Africa to form a policy with a limited number of very strong partnerships rather than a much larger number of shallow ones. While shallow pairings are necessary, they cannot be forged at the cost of diverting attention from the need to cultivate very strong partnerships. The social fabric in India has wrinkles that sometimes lead to African students studying in institutions in the country becoming the subject of bigoted comments. However, India has, overall, favourably impacted the young population of a continent that is as destined for greatness in this century as Asia was in the previous. More students from the African continent need to be attracted to study in universities and institutes in India, and the effort needs to be to move towards the acceptance of the Indian rupee as a mode of exchange among more African countries, as was the case pre-Independence and even after it, for a while, before the Nehru-era central planning impacted such transactions. Anglospheric countries, such as Kenya and South Africa, have the potential to become strong partners in India's moves to ensure the effective, and not just formal, independence of African countries that are being pressurized by known countries to alter their policies in a manner that benefits only the latter, if not immediately, then in the medium to long term.

'Win-win' has often been used as a catchphrase by a country that follows a 'heads I win, tails you lose' mentality, and closer ties with India will help African countries ensure that the policy paths that they take finally benefit them and not outside powers seeking to dominate them in practice while crooning to them in theory. This is particularly true of the PRC. Just as South Africa and Kenya are prominent building blocks in the architecture needed to ensure a free and open Indo-Pacific, so is the Republic of Madagascar. Should the country adopt a few of the tried-and-tested reforms to promote faster growth, it has the potential to emerge as a powerhouse in Africa, the way Japan and now Taiwan have risen in Asia. Although, Taiwan has not fully recovered from the shock it suffered when Kissinger threw away its interests in his acceptance of the conditions for normalization with China, most of which were proffered as a negotiating gambit by the Chinese side.

AMERICAN UNRELIABILITY AND INDIAN AUTONOMY

Beijing was so aware of its own vulnerabilities vis-à-vis the USSR that Kissinger had no need to surrender the honour of the US in the manner that he (with the assent of President Nixon) did in the case of Taiwan. Such craven behaviour is uncommon for the US, although President Trump's surrender to the Taliban, sacrificing the interests and endangering the survival of the elected government in Kabul, is another example of a shift in policy that seriously damaged the credibility of the US as a stable long-term partner.

Another such example is the way in which the Kurds were pushed under the bus, again, by Trump, to appease President Erdoğan of Turkey, brave verbiage notwithstanding. Although President Trump did finally sanction Turkey under CAATSA for its purchase of the S-400 system from Russia, he simply did this because it was mandatory under US law to do so. Trump imposed relatively mild sanctions in the expectation that the slap on the wrist would be the entirety of the punishment suffered by Ankara for abandoning obligations as a member of NATO, even as another administration could take charge in the 2020 presidential polls, as, indeed, did happen.

President Biden could follow the example of Trump and either ignore or be casual about the CAATSA sanctions on the countries buying and installing equipment. This would make the operations of the US or US-made platforms problematic in the theatres involved. Consequently, the Sino-Russian alliance would dominate the weapons market in coming years by driving out competition from the US and the EU through managed prices and loan schemes that are tempting at first but reveal their toxicity later.

Strategic independence does not mean the avoidance of a partnership with the US and with countries formed from the same security grid as Washington such as Japan, France or Australia. It means the need to differentiate between a relationship that is similar to what took place in Eastern European countries through the instrumentality of the Warsaw Pact, and to an extent, some of the agreements that Washington forged in Asia. Those who entered into such pacts needed to accept the security imperatives, and even the foreign policy initiatives of the USSR or the US, although this was conflicting with their own interests. India is sui generis in the way the PRC or the US are, and it has the necessary geopolitical heft to ensure that its policies remain independent even within an alliance, the way Charles de Gaulle or Jacques Chirac ensured France remained independent. Hence, India needs to deepen ties with Iran, ignoring the advice to the contrary from Washington. This deepening can include, through the setting up of payment systems, using the rupee rather than the dollar as the unit of exchange (at first, partially, but later, completely). Such trade in local currencies can get used in situations where one of the partners has lost access to hard currency due to financial sanctions.

CONNECTING WITH SOUTH AMERICA

A South American country that India needs to establish close ties with is Venezuela. This can be done by purchasing oil from Venezuela. Those in the US who sought a return to the days prior to the civil rights legislation of President Lyndon Johnson in the 1960s regard the efforts by some leaders in South America to ensure greater justice to indigenous communities as anathema. Such individuals do not consider people from these communities as full human beings and certainly not those with even a fraction of the rights that they deserve to enjoy in their respective countries, which lacked them for a considerable period of time. For example, Hugo Chávez made the mistake of Robert Mugabe in Zimbabwe in looking at society in purely racial terms, much as their detractors had.

Whether in the case of South Africa, or earlier, in the case of India, it must not be forgotten than many white people backed the cause of freedom and justice for those who were being oppressed and who were of a different race than their white oppressors. Zimbabwe and Venezuela have paid a heavy societal and economic price by policies designed to discriminate, often severely, against those who had long practised racial superiority on the indigenous populations of countries in South America and Africa. In that sense, South Africa, under Nelson Mandela, adopted a more sensible policy. Admittedly, the progress of social justice in South Africa has been slow and needs to be accelerated, but, overall, the difference between the policies of President Mandela and those of President Mugabe have made a considerable difference in the trajectories of South Africa and Zimbabwe, respectively. Reverse racism has helped neither Zimbabwe nor Venezuela, and certainly, this is a lesson that needs to be learnt by those who seek to fight prejudice with prejudice, injustice with injustice.

India needs to identify with the aspirations of indigenous communities in South America for justice and progress in their lives within the context of the Mandela Model, which does not seek to fight one form of racism with another. Human society is not vertical but horizontal. It is not that some are superior to others. Each human being is equal in quality and potential. The only factors that differentiate humans are the extent to which they have opportunities for positive development and the extent to which they take advantage of such doors to personal and social advancement.

The other country in the region with which an effort to create a close working relationship needs to be made is Mexico. This is a country that lost territory to the US in the past, but it has since witnessed a continuing flow of its sons and daughters across the Rio Grande. The Stephen Miller project of seeking to perpetuate into the indefinite future the majority population of the US remaining white has negated the fact that 'all men are created equal.' The Mexican-American and indeed the Latino community in the US has the vibrancy of a talented people and is an asset to the US rather than the liability that the Trump administration imagined them to be. Mexico has a history that goes back thousands of years. It is a civilization that predates the arrival of Spanish fortune hunters, who set upon the indigenous population in a manner that made a mockery of their claim to be followers of the Christian faith, which totally disapproves of the acts of brutality that were inflicted by the invaders on the indigenous population in 1521.

Understanding and celebrating the roots of a civilization is essential to building a healthy spirit of nationhood. India and Mexico are linked together in such an endeavour. Whether it is Mexico or Brazil—a country that is already close to India—the importance of doing justice to indigenous peoples and retrieving their history to include them in the overall narrative taught to its youth is a shared value that India can and does relate to with warmth. Even in the US, greater outreach needs to be made to the Latino community, for they are similar to the people of India in having a long historical past that was sought to be buried by its colonizers.

This is a short list that has not (except in some cases, in passing) mentioned countries with which India has already developed close relations, such as Vietnam or Singapore in Asia. Rather, it focusses on countries where a special effort needs to be made to accelerate bilateral relationships. Among the other priorities is the need to forge partnerships with the smaller island nations of the Indo-Pacific, principally the Kingdom of Tonga, which, in terms of its soft power, is the most influential among the group of island states it belongs to. South Asia is a special case, which will be dealt with in the next chapter.

7

India in Its Immediate Neighbourhood

The Pakistan establishment alters its history[1] to argue that its civilization stretches back centuries, not to other parts of the Indian subcontinent, as is the case, but, in different accounts, to Turkey, Afghanistan, Central Asia and even the Arab world. The purpose behind this revisionism is instilling within the psyche and emotions of the people that they share neither historical nor cultural roots with India. The conclusions so awkwardly drawn are that the DNA of Pakistan, in spite of it eagerly joining the South Asian Association for Regional Cooperation (SAARC), has nothing to do with South Asia but, in fact, is a mixture of Turkish, Arabic and Central Asian DNA. Such researches are no surprise, for Pakistan has long sought to distance itself from South Asia.[2] The only link that GHQ Rawalpindi is adamant on retaining with South Asia is the continued membership in the SAARC as a destructive disruptor. This is because it serves the interests of the country to which the military in Pakistan has tethered its fate—China.

From the beginning, as a SAARC member, Pakistan's approach has been seeking to stifle whatever green shoots of cooperation that are generated within the administrative and diplomatic machinery of an alliance that this country has rendered inoperable wherever it gets involved. Pakistan has been pressing with particular vehemence that the PRC should be included as a full member of the club. Beijing gives loud hints every now and again that it would be open to accepting such a friendly offer. While a case may be made that Tibet is linked more to South Asia than to other parts of China, overall, the PRC is as much a part of South Asia as is Greenland.

The PRC abuts the east coast of the Eurasian landmass. Its border with the rest of South Asia is of relatively recent vintage and has been secured through its seizure of Tibet in the 1950s and control over parts of Ladakh and Kashmir that were illegally seized by Pakistan, despite the state having acceded to India. The fact that the PRC is considered as much or more South Asian than India by the generals in Pakistan is another example of the propensity of the Pakistan military to substitute fiction for fact—a trait it shares with its ally, the PRC.[3] The early inclusion of Myanmar into the SAARC would be far more logical, for the country has much in common in its culture, history as well as its interests with the present members of SAARC minus the Turkish-Arab-Central Asian combo that mythmakers in Pakistan want the country to appear to be to the outside world, except, of course, when SAARC meetings take place.

AMERICAN DECISIVENESS

From the beginning of the Cold War 1.0, Washington (correctly looking at its own interests) framed its policy to hasten the demise of the USSR. Soviet leaders, from Nikita Khruschev to Alexei Kosygin and, most insistently, Gorbachev, at different times, believed that this behaviour would change, that the US as well as its partners across the Atlantic would assist the USSR to not just tide over its difficulties but to thrive. Yeltsin handed over policymaking to a group of individuals who followed the US's advice about what was best for their country, especially in economic policy. In other words, they implemented policies that were designed to do what the US Treasury Secretary Henry Morgenthau sought for Germany in 1944 after World War II was over—pastoralizing Germany by forcibly converting it into a producer of raw materials.

Morgenthau's plan would have dismantled Germany's industrial and technological base. However, Roosevelt's death ensured that the US quickly returned to the post-1917 policy of regarding Moscow as the enemy to watch out for, something which got Berlin (or Bonn, at the time) off the hook. In the eastern quadrant of Germany, which came under the control of the USSR, many industrial units were shifted eastwards into the USSR, while several of the diminished state's scientists and technologists were relocated to cities in the USSR. However, after Stalin's death in 1953, this policy was scrapped, principally because the three quadrants of Germany that fell under the control of France, the UK and the US soon saw industry begin to flourish in what became known as the Federal Republic of Germany, while the German Democratic Republic (GDR), which was under the control of the USSR, visibly lagged behind. East Germany never caught up with West Germany in economic parameters, although, by the close of the 1960s, the GDR was doing much better than most other Soviet bloc countries.

GANDHI'S FAST AND INDIA'S FORGIVENESS

In contrast to the hard-nosed and unsentimental setting of US policy towards an adversary, it was taken for granted in India that the oft-quoted mantra of a strong Pakistan being in India's interests was accurate rather than what it ought to have been seen as—an attempt at mordant humour. India took the cue for a policy of serially forgiving the depredations of Pakistan from Mahatma Gandhi, who undertook a fast unto death that he ended only when the government, led by Nehru, with Sardar Patel as his deputy, gave a substantial sum of money to Pakistan.[4] Although the Mahatma did not know this, his fast effectively became a death warrant because it motivated Nathuram Vinayak Godse to assassinate him on 30 January 1948. This is clear in Godse's final declaration before the court pronounced the death sentence for him.[5]

Successive PMs sought to follow in the saintly path of the Mahatma, regardless of what Pakistan had done in the interregnum to damage India's interests. This, in the view of the Lutyens Zone, gave Pakistan successive chances to redeem itself through gratitude for yet another act of sublime generosity from India. Whether at Tashkent in 1966, at Shimla in 1972 or the way in which the Pakistan Army was allowed to escape from the trap it had laid for itself in Kargil in 1999, the post-Independence policy of giving substantive concessions to Pakistan for mere promises of good behaviour in the future was followed. There were a few who, from the 1980s, insisted that this policy of automatic absolution and forgiveness of GHQ Rawalpindi was flawed and needed to be replaced. Such views started to be taken seriously only after Modi took over as the PM on 26 May 2014, and saw for himself, in his initial years in office, what should have been obvious to his predecessors—Pakistan was regularly pocketing each of the concessions India made, complaining that they were not enough and immediately returning to its earlier troublesome behaviour. The search by Indian interlocutors to prise open, through compromise, the softer side of the generals of GHQ Rawalpindi has remained a futile but oft-repeated enterprise.

DECOUPLING COMMERCE AND ARMS

A societally healthy Pakistan, with a governance system that frees itself from servitude to a military with no visible limit to the depredations that it is willing to inflict on its targets, would indeed be welcome. The same has never been the case with a country that is under the control of GHQ Rawalpindi. Over the decades, the phrase 'a strong Pakistan' has been code for a strong military, when the reality is that the latter is a parasite feeding on the former. The more resources and policy space it sucks in, the more the interests of the people of Pakistan are harmed. Whether it be the US or the PRC, assistance to Islamabad has meant help to the military in (a) retaining its control over the civilian establishment and (b) boosting its destructive capabilities in the continuing conflict with India.

To argue, as Washington did in the past and Beijing does now, that assistance in supplying offensive weaponry to Pakistan is not directed against India is false, and the US and the PRC know this. The advantage they have is the absence of anything other than a verbal reaction from India at such kinetic assistance to a military whose sole mission is the meltdown of India. Beyond a point that was long ago breached by the PLA, such help needed to impact the overall Sino-Indian relationship, including commerce. That it had not done so for so long is a reflection of the propensity of policymakers in India to continue with lines of action that have long ceased to be of value to the national interest. Only after the May 2020 incursions has some action been taken on the commerce front. During 2021–22, the surplus of China in its trade with India crossed $90 billion, and is closing in on $100 billion annually.[6] A few steps have been taken, for example, in the case of online applications, and preventing Chinese telecom companies from dominating the 5G space in India, the way they do in the related fields of telecom.

The measures implemented since the 2020 Sino-Indian border clashes by PM Modi were needed and must be enhanced. Such a decoupling ought to have begun at least a decade ago, when it had become clear within the portals of Indian intelligence agencies that Xi had begun to put PRC expansionism on a fast track, at the expense of India. Despite its hostile policies, the attraction of Indian business to easy money through the destruction of domestic production in India by importing PRC substitutes continues.[7] In a situation where companies from the US, Japan and Taiwan in particular are seeking to relocate from China, such a high level of dependence on China of several businesspersons in India does not inspire confidence in the depth of commitment of India towards ensuring that the Indo-Pacific, as indeed the Eurasian landmass, are protected from the domination of the PRC.[8]

RESCUING PAKISTAN FOR INDIAN INTERESTS

The effort by the international community, including India, ought to be bringing Pakistan to a healthy state by seeking to secure, through sanctions on key individuals in the military and by other means, the withdrawal of the men in khaki from within the inner councils of what is inaccurately termed the civilian Government of Pakistan—a construct that governs very little. This is why both the US and the PRC concentrate their attention on the Pakistan military. Only a dialogue and understanding with them has any chance of having the commitments of Pakistan in such interactions be carried out. Unless such a change occurs, it is not in the interests of India (nor indeed the US or the EU) to boost the Pakistan military, which has been expertly camouflaging, for the sake of external donors, money used by it as assistance to the people of Pakistan or to the civilian government of the country. In particular, the nationalities in Pakistan need to regain their self-respect by securing equal treatment from policymakers in Islamabad, an impossibility as long as GHQ Rawalpindi is in command of the governance system.

The Pakistan military is dominated by the Punjab province, that too mainly by those from Pothwar.[9] To make Pakistan stable, justice needs to be served to the Sindhi, Baloch and Shia minority and Pashtun population of the country. This will not happen as long as a military dominated by a single ethnic group runs the country. Considerations of justice and fair play mandate global support for enhancing the presently pitiable level of rights for such minorities in Pakistan, not to mention the fate of women at the hands of the Wahhabi clergy that has long been indulged by the military. Supporting the rights of nationalities in Pakistan that have faced discrimination on a rising scale since Zia-ul-Haq's advent to power does not mean that the breakup of Pakistan has been backed. It means the opposite, pointing to the only way that country can avoid a meltdown. The centrifugal tensions and pressures caused by systemic discrimination are leading to a meltdown of the State, and the only way to rescue the situation is to ensure justice to such elements.

It is within such a context that India needs to proactively form an international coalition designed not to break up Pakistan but to save Pakistan from the religious bigots and domination by a single section of an ethnic group that is tearing the country apart by dominating over other groups. Those in Pakistan who are fighting oppression enforced through the military need to be provided refuge and a platform by India rather than be left to fend for themselves against a predatory force that has long had a single mission—wreck the future of India while ensuring the denial of such rights and freedoms to its people that are commonplace in genuine democracies. So far as SAARC is concerned, the ability of a forum that is being actively subverted by a single member to be effective in implementing stated objectives is limited. Structures that (temporarily) exclude Pakistan need to be created. Whether bilateral, trilateral or multilateral, there needs to be engagement between India and the other members of SAARC barring Pakistan, thus freeing such institutions of internal sabotage.

UNREQUITED GENEROSITY FOR ENEMIES

Until 1971, Bangladesh has endured the ethnic discrimination and other harmful attentions of the Wahhabized military of Pakistan. The Government of India should have been firm at the 1972 Shimla conference with the defeated power that at least a few dozen officers of the men of the Pakistan Army would be made to stand trial on charges of genocide, rape and other atrocities. Rather than shifting all the 93,000 prisoners of war of the Pakistan Army to camps in India, the authorities taking charge in Bangladesh ought to have been given the opportunity of examining the conduct of the captured soldiers during the previous years, and separated those who have been confirmed to be guilty of war crimes—through a credible process—from the rest. Such criminals needed to be tried in Bangladesh in special courts set up for the purpose.

Generosity to deadly enemies has long been a trait among the ruling elites of India from the time of Prithviraj Chauhan a millennium ago. PM Indira Gandhi sacrificed an advantage, when she lost at Shimla in 1972 what Field Marshal Sam Manekshaw had won for her on the battlefield in 1971. A substantial disservice was done to the cause of protecting humanity from depredators by the way in which an instant pardon was given by the Indian side to every Pakistani soldier in its custody. Trials for war criminals would have established a record of the reasons why intervention in Bangladesh became necessary despite the joint opposition of Beijing and Washington. Such trials would have deepened the education of the people of the new country in the blood-soaked history preceding its formation. Instead, the interests of justice were ignored for the hundreds of thousands killed by the Pakistan military and the millions who had been made refugees by the actions of the same force. This was unfair both to Bangladesh and its people as well as to the traditions and principles that are expected to be promoted rather than ignored by India. The 'get out of jail without penalty' pass given to the Pakistan Army ensured not merely the subsequent coup against the victor of Shimla, Zulfikar Ali Bhutto and his subsequent murder, but the revival of the Wahhabi fringe and sympathizers and collaborators of the Pakistan military in Bangladesh, who killed Sheikh Mujibur Rahman and diverted the country from the secular course that the Bangabandhu was setting the new country on.

An aspect that needs attention is the treatment of minorities by radicalized sections of the majority community in Bangladesh. Rather than taking them into India, these minorities need to be protected by the government of the day in Dhaka, and this is what Indian diplomacy ought to attempt. Not doing so, and simply admitting them into India, is a policy born of despair that the religious supremacy practised by many in Bangladesh cannot be controlled and eliminated. Such an attitude towards other faiths is an abomination, no matter what the country or the faith may be. Whether it is Bangabandhu Sheikh Mujibur Rahman or the 'Frontier Gandhi' Khan Abdul Gaffar Khan, such heroes of the subcontinent need to be celebrated in India. Doing so would not simply strengthen their legacies in their home countries, but boost better people-to-people relations between India and Bangladesh.

India's relations with Afghanistan and Bangladesh are not on the same level as Pakistan, which is why it was a surprise to Kabul as well as Dhaka to find them tagged along with Islamabad in the Citizenship (Amendment) Act (CAA), 2019.[10] Both PM Modi and PM Sheikh Hasina have succeeded in erasing several of the earlier blockages affecting cooperation between the two countries. Transportation links have been strengthened, and the people on both sides are beginning to understand the value of cooperation. Within South Asia, good relations between any of the countries in the grouping and India are helpful to economic growth, and this is a principle that has been operationalized by both sides. A similar dynamic is at play between India and Afghanistan.

WAHHABISM AND AMERICA

During the initial years of the Trump presidency, it appeared that the global campaign to ensure the rollback of Wahhabism was finally getting support from a US administration that has historically empowered Wahhabis to meet some short-term tactical need. This has led to an expansion in the dominance of this fringe, even within institutions serving the Muslim mainstream, which is moderate and where the youth, in particular, are inclined towards embracing rather than rejecting modernity. This would not be obvious from much of the visual and print media in major democracies, which effectively accept the erroneous proposition that most Muslims go by the dictates of that fringe and its preachers. Almost all 'Muslim' voices that get highlighted in the media in major democracies such as the US, the UK and often, India as well, come from the Wahhabi fringe rather than from the moderate mainstream. The consequence is that a view has gained ground internationally that the majority of Muslims favour the exclusivist doctrines that are the staple of the Wahhabi International and its Khomeinist cousin. This has generated often severe forms of Islamophobia, in a world where people of all faiths need to be regarded and treated equally. Until there is a rollback of the expansion of influence of the Wahhabi International, in particular, security and societal stability are at risk in an interdependent world.

Sadly, on 15 August 2021, President Biden followed the 1996 example of President Clinton and installed the Taliban in power in Kabul, after his country had gone to war in 2001 to remove it from power. This retrogressive step by Biden is likely to have the same consequences as what took place during the first stint of the Taliban in power. The devastation of 9/11 followed from that action, and members of Wahhabi terror groups, once again, have a safe haven in Afghanistan. Champagne may have popped in GHQ Rawalpindi on this occasion, but that glee is likely to be short-lived. Pashtun assertion has been put on steroids by the Taliban defeating the US, and this is likely to create a Balochistan-type situation in the Pashtun-majority areas of Pakistan. These are chafing under the control of the Punjabi-dominated military, and are likely to challenge the authority of the men in khaki in their country. Given the links that bind Pashtuns together, it is doubtful whether the Taliban (despite the presence of several agents of the Pakistan military in it)[11] will make any serious effort to restrain their fellow Pashtuns south of the Durand Line. Rather, much of the Taliban may assist Pashtuns in Pakistan to use the usual methods in that part of the world and wrest freedom from control by the men in khaki.

President Trump had his drawbacks and has made more than a few mistakes. However, the White House, during his tenure, gave an impetus to modernizers, such as MBS of Saudi Arabia and Khalifa bin Zayed al-Nayhan from the United Arab Emirates (UAE). Both Saudi Arabia as well as the UAE have worked to roll back the scaffolding of the Wahhabi version of a noble faith that threatens the future of the young, and thereby the very existence of these and other states. PM Modi has reached out to both these modernizers, and with their help, has improved the relationship between India and Saudi Arabia as well as with the UAE under the futuristic leadership of both. Sadly, Trump diluted the strength of the attempted rollback of Wahhabism in 2019 by supporting the current leader of the Wahhabi fringe, President Erdoğan of Turkey, in forcing the Kurdish fighters who had been instrumental in the war against the Islamic State of Iraq and Syria (ISIS) to withdraw from their fortified positions. Thereby, those who trusted the US and worked alongside its military in seeking to defeat a common foe were betrayed, much as the Czechs had been in 1938 by Chamberlain and Daladier.

In 2020, President Trump surrendered the interests of an ally yet again to a Wahhabi force, when he signed an agreement with the Taliban which, once implemented, would plunge

Afghanistan into chaos and bloodshed on a scale not seen since 2001. It is clear that the numerous sympathizers of China and Pakistan within the Biden establishment perhaps played a key role in convincing the unwary US President that it was not just in the US interest but also in his own political interest to scurry away from Afghanistan in the pell-mell manner that Biden ordered in 2021. Earlier, the elected government in Kabul was forced by the Trump administration to release more than 3,000 Taliban fighters, who had been captured at great cost to Afghan lives. The US's action has led to a sharp increase in the Afghan lives being lost, and is likely to have the same effect on the lives of US troops in the years to come, now that the Taliban have formed the government in Kabul. This was intended by Trump when the Doha Agreement was signed between the US government and the Taliban in 2020, to the exclusion of the legitimate government of Afghanistan.

8

Hard Choices, Never Soft Options

India's relative underperformance on so many parameters, such as the annual rate of growth of the economy or per capita income, may be related to the obsession with designing and implementing soft options, for example, in foreign policy, when the reality of Cold War 1.0 between the USSR and the US was, in effect, ignored by successive leaders of the country. This is why economic reform has been such a difficult process to implement in India. What is considered a soft option in a year can become progressively harder for the country. Conversely, what seems like, and often is, the hard option in the immediate future (which, in the minds of politicians, is the next election cycle), may bring substantial benefits at a later date.

The few hard options that have been implemented have usually come at the beginning of an administration when, after an election, elected governments usually have a window during which oversight by the vanquished Opposition is far lower than would be the case later in the term. Consequently, after token gestures from the Opposition to register disapproval, such hard reforms can be implemented. This was the situation between 1991 and 1993, the first two years of the Narasimha Rao government, or in the afterglow of the Kargil fightback, a year after Vajpayee successfully secured a majority for the NDA in the 1999 polls. Despite the failure to prevent the Pakistan military from occupying the Kargil heights, which the Indian military should never have descended from, the Indian Air Force and the Indian Army managed to resist against GHQ Rawalpindi's plan to capture the Kargil range and won it back from Pakistan.

PM Modi had a clear field for a little more than the first two years of his first term (2014–19) but chose to move cautiously on the economic front during this period. Another chance came his way after he successfully secured a second term with a greater majority in 2019, but the onset of the Covid-19 pandemic in 2020 created headwinds that boosted the confidence of the Opposition that 2024 will be different from 2014 and 2019. From the end of 2020, the Opposition has intensified efforts at downgrading the performance of the Modi government, in the expectation that such an outcome would reduce the BJP's chances of securing a hat-trick in its 2024 electoral performance. It is, of course, true that perceptions need a link with the reality being experienced by the audience that is being appealed to. Should the connect between what is known as 'spin' or 'hype' be faint, efforts at creating perceptions will fail in the hustings. In 2019, voters were yet to lose hope in Modi, someone who would beneficially change in their lives, but by 2024, hope will be replaced by experience. Should the latter not meet the standards of the former, there will be blowback. Should hope and reality mesh, any spin or hype in the opposite directions by political groups will fail. Regardless of the 2024 election results, New Delhi needs to focus on long-term choices that seem hard now but are beneficial in the long run rather than short-term soft options.

DIPLOMACY IN THE NEIGHBOURHOOD

Much ado has been made about India's 'need' to 'ensure a stable neighbourhood' and 'increase its regional influence' before the country can ascend to a global or even a continental power. In the first place, India's role in the trajectory of most of its neighbours is limited by capacity and circumstance. Rather than expend effort in tasks that are often quixotic in nature and scope, what would be better is for the government to concentrate on economic development and its attendant benefits of high growth rates that include increased societal stability and security from external threats. Although this has been portrayed as the goal of diplomacy since the time of Narasimha Rao, as is commonplace with policymaking in the Lutyens Zone, action has seldom come close to rhetoric. Self-goals, such as the ones set as part of the clumsily named CAA, 2019, have continued. The CAA created an easier pathway to citizenship for those of specific faiths from specific countries while excluding the rest. Given the trauma that the subcontinent has already suffered in the past and continues to experience in the present as a consequence of the Two-Nation theory, it is unfortunate that inclusion and exclusion in the law was made on the basis of religious affiliation. There are those who have been pampered by some regimes while others have been excoriated, and both lists include people of multiple faiths.

Equally importantly, India needs to expend diplomatic and other efforts in ensuring that any persecution of minorities by regimes (especially in the military controlled governance structure of Pakistan) be opposed and sought to be reversed. The passing of the CAA will be taken as a green light by zealots in Pakistan and Bangladesh, besides, of course, Afghanistan, to continue their longstanding efforts at changing the demographic profile of their countries. The CAA is likely to have the opposite effect of what its framers claimed to intend, which is the protection of the rights of minorities in certain countries bordering India (and not others). Overall, the law seems to have had a clear religious focus, which is a problem in a subcontinent that has been the victim of the common, irrational tendency to regard those of another faith as coming from a different planet.

The inclusion of Afghanistan and Bangladesh together with Pakistan was another problematic feature of the CAA. Both Afghanistan and Bangladesh are friends of India in a manner that Pakistan has not been allowed to be by the military in Pakistan since 1947. Thus, including these two countries with an obvious foe of India was less than helpful in the essential task of building better relations with them in the context of the increased synchronization of several moves on India by Islamabad and Beijing. This is obvious but bears repetition.

FRINGE ELEMENTS AND SOFT OPTIONS

Any measure or messaging that widens the fringe in any section of the population, shrinking the moderate middle in the process, needs to be avoided and, indeed, resisted by policymakers. This is why it is important to classify certain crimes, such as killing an individual for eating the meat of certain types of the bovine population, as terrorist acts. In the first place, democracies should not use the bludgeon of law to effect lifestyles changes related to diet, dress or sexual orientation. These are matters of the kitchen and the bedroom not within the provenance of the State. It is true that some countries that ban particular types of dress, lifestyle or diet (often on pain of death) seem to not be garnering the attention that India has from some members of the international community for hate crimes based on the opposition to the choices of some citizens. This is because the world's largest democracy is held up to higher—much higher—standards than others. Of course, those who assume that India was heaven before 26 May 2014, when Modi was sworn in as the PM, and became a hell immediately thereafter are as wrong as those who believe that life was hell before that date and has become heaven thereafter.

Historically, it may be said that Mahatma Gandhi's backing of the Khilafat Movement (1919–24) gave life to the fringe sections of the Muslim community, at the expense of the middle. Carrying forward this legacy, PM Nehru sought to lock the stable doors after the 'horse' of Partition had already bolted. He avoided reforming laws related to Muslims and, overall, sought to craft laws specific to the Hindu community (such as the Hindu Code Bill or, later, the Right to Education Act) that effectively treated Hindus in the manner that minorities have been treated in so many countries. Temples remained in the control of the State, whereas the places of worship of other faiths were spared of government control. Furthermore, Hindus have been subjected to laws and procedures that discriminate against them, a practice carried out with zeal by the INC during the Sonia Gandhi–Manmohan Singh decade. For example, the Right to Education Act exempts educational institutions run by members of the minority communities of any obligations and places obligations only on institutions run by the majority community. This has severely impacted the relative share of new institutions set up by members of the majority community in a context where the burden of sharing social costs needed to be equalized for all.

Feeding the fringe seldom makes for good politics, as this group is impossible to satisfy unless one completely surrenders to their demands at the expense of the rest of society. Secularism implies equal treatment to those of all faiths rather than differential treatment in legal and administrative practice. The British-era policy of the colonial state seizing control of Hindu temples while not doing the same with the places of worship of other communities is an aberration that has been toxic to the development of a genuinely secular mindset in India.[1] This and other such aberrations remain unrectified. To seek to somehow compensate for them through initiating policies that appear to discriminate against the minorities is equally erroneous. Such practices will neither help the internal stability of India nor its external influence. At the same time, unnecessary irritants, such as a ban on hijab in a college in Karnataka in February 2022,[2] need to be avoided, even as any attempts to make wearing items such as the niqab or the burka compulsory in schools and colleges should be stopped.

The removal of Article 370 from the Constitution of India and the subsequent changes in the manner in which the former state of Jammu and Kashmir was governed failed to gain popular traction among those who opposed it. While unsuccessful in India, such elements made more progress in countries that had, in the past, sided with Pakistan on the Kashmir issue, with parliamentarians and even the PM of Malaysia and a Canadian MP, who disapproved of India's efforts to beat back attempts at further vivisecting the region, once again, on the grounds of religion.[3] The geopolitical heft of India and the essentiality of its inclusion in any strategy by the US and its allies ensured that such voices found few takers apart from those with linkages to the Pakistan establishment.

NATIONAL DECISIONS, INTERNATIONAL REPUTATION

The Indian Agriculture Acts of 2020, commonly known as the three Farm Bills, were a different matter. Who the principal strategists behind the agitation to force the withdrawal of these Acts were is still unclear. What is clear is that a strategy of portraying the legislation as 'anti-farmer' picked up traction rapidly in Punjab as well as in parts of Rajasthan, Uttar Pradesh and Haryana. Had the agitation demanding the withdrawal of the three Acts been nipped in the bud during the first few weeks, or at the most within a month of its onset, the Government of India may have been able to contain the situation. However, once the agitators were convinced that the police were under instructions to avoid using force, the protests snowballed. By the end of 2020, they had finally reached a level of farmer participation (mainly from Punjab) that emboldened supporters of the movement to not relent on their demands.

A move like this can lead to the credibility of the government as an instrument of reform plummeting across the world. Investors respect those who make hard choices. However, in the case of the Farm Bills, from the start, it was apparent that hard options were going to be avoided despite the consequence that acceding to the demand for withdrawal could severely damage the image of the government. It is not unusual for the soft option to create the most damage to a government's interests—a situation that the soft option was presumed to obviate.

Despite his defeat in the 1996 polls, the reforms carried out by Narasimha Rao cemented his standing in the history of India as an outstanding leader. At a later date, Vajpayee's reforms did the same for the first BJP PM. Narasimha Rao's reforms have been blamed for his defeat. However, in the final years of his tenure, the process of additional economic reform slowed down to a crawl, which could be attributed to the blowback from the voters, especially in the Hindi belt. Furthermore, what cemented his defeat was his refusal to proceed with what could have been popular and necessary steps in his final years. This includes canning another peaceful nuclear explosion, although India had both the capacity and the need to proceed with it. Again, he chose the soft option of avoiding such a provocation, even though such a move could have drawn the attention of those minds in global chancelleries that were dismissing India as a second-rate power.

The 2014 and 2019 Lok Sabha polls were converted by Modi into a presidential contest, the first between Sonia Gandhi and himself and the next between him and Rahul Gandhi. It remains to be seen who his principal challenger will be in 2024, but what is not in doubt is that systemic reforms would improve rather than lower his chances for a victory. Similarly, innovations in foreign policy are taking place on a scale not seen in the economic portfolios, and several are likely to remain permanent, even if there is a change in government.

KEEPING INDIAN ALLIES CLOSE

While Covid-19, together with the condition of the economy, form the biggest domestic challenges confronting PM Modi, the foreign and security policy challenge is ensuring an adequate level of protection against what he has described as 'expansionism' in several of his speeches.[4] This involves not only working together with the US and many of its long-standing allies, such as the UK, France, Japan and Australia, but also with countries like Vietnam and Indonesia. At the same time, India's much prized 'strategic autonomy' needs to be used in the case of countries, such as Venezuela and Iran, that have been at the receiving end of US-led efforts at a regime change by systematically collapsing their economies through sanctions. Even when such efforts, which were at a particularly high pitch during the tenure of President Trump, are paused, Washington needs a Plan B in case its efforts at regime change or drastic changes in regime policy fail. A working relationship between such countries and India could become as asset for the US should there be an adverse change in circumstances.

Damaged relations between countries always result in mutual or one-sided losses. For example, when Hugo Chávez turned his back on the US, the largest market for crude oil—the single biggest export of Venezuela—the economy and, consequently, the funding for social justice policy, began to slide in Venezuela.[5] Another example is Iran. If the corridor linking the Chabahar port to Central Asia and Afghanistan becomes operational, friendly ties between Tehran and New Delhi, fuelled by resuming the purchase of oil (as well as the expeditious completion of the rail and road links to the port from these locations), could ensure that the US supplies to Afghanistan and Central Asia have a route other than the one cutting through Pakistan. On multiple occasions, Islamabad (or rather, GHQ Rawalpindi) has not hesitated to blackmail Washington by threatening to cut off this route. Should an alternative route become available, courtesy India, with the tacit or open consent of Iran, the concessions made as a result of such pressure would largely cease. Iran would itself benefit greatly: first, by an increase in the use of the route and second, from the reduced tensions caused by such a gesture to the US. Iran and the US regard the Wahhabi resurgence in Afghanistan and Central Asia as worrisome, despite the mutual demonology claiming that the other has the opposite policy, while Trump's withdrawal from the JCPOA has only increased Tehran's dependence on Beijing, just as President Bush boosted Tehran's influence in Baghdad after he carried out the 2003 War of Freedom in Iraq. India can be instrumental in effectuating this improvement in relations.

France is a country that has stood with India consistently, even during the choppy period after the Pokhran II nuclear tests in 1998, which resembles what the USSR did from the 1950s, until its demise in 1991. This sets France apart from the UK, whose support during times of crisis has often been either tepid or hostile, as seen during the 1965 war launched by Ayub Khan against India, in which we were led by Lal Bahadur Shastri. London ought to have understood the consequences of seeking to replace India with the artificial construct of Pakistan long ago, but influential segments of the policymaking community in London still cling to their long-standing prejudice against India. However, what may be termed the traditionalist 'Raab' strain—named after Dominic Raab, the deputy PM of the UK—appears to be giving way to the more pragmatic 'Boris' variety—named after Boris Johnson, the PM of the UK—in the Conservative Party, with Labour still mired in the Harold Wilson period of the tilt against India.

As for Germany, its dealings with Russia and China indicate that their policy is based on (short-term) commercial needs rather than being firmly anchored within the context of the tectonic shifts in geopolitics that are taking place in 2021–22, which are nowhere close to being similar to the changes in 1880–81, 1990–91 or even 2010–11. The current logic of events is driving the process that guides, or ought to guide, policymaking.

The policymaking matrices in the US, Russia, Australia, Japan and even China have changed. The same needs to happen in India. These changes need to be comprehensive rather than, as has been the tradition in the Lutyens Zone, segmented into silos, with action by one often leading to a dilution in the effectiveness of the action taken by another. The higher reaches of government need to set a correct direction for our policymaking matrix rather than working towards all-round control.

STEPS FOR A PROSPEROUS FUTURE

The rise of the UK as the pre-eminent global power was not the result of a conscious strategy implemented from the top. Rather, it was the consequence of its ruling elite giving its citizens the freedom to think and act. A collection of individual actions, discoveries and conquests coalesced into the British Empire. Centralized states, such as Spain or France, during that time had no chance of matching the success of the British Empire. An increasing number of people from the lower levels of society found their way to the middle, and some even discovered pathways to the top of the food chain. Only that society is healthy where a middle class grows proportionately to the lower classes—a middle class from which several manage to migrate upwards in terms of income and achievement. An all of government approach is indeed the panacea.

In terms of international relations, the MEA needs effective steps from the defence, home, commerce and finance ministries to achieve success in its efforts at improving the diplomatic footprint of India. Whether all elements in the official machinery understand that India is engaged in a war with a power that battles on several fronts may be a matter of debate, judging by some policy actions and responses. It is not known whether every element in the government accepts that policymakers need to get over the delusion that balanced relationships should always be the goal, even when such a stance may be in opposition to the national interest.

What is clear is that the average citizen knows that this is war and that in Cold War 2.0, India stands with the democracies against the extremism of religious supremacists and the expansionism of autocracies. Those who have led India have almost always pulled away from exploiting the consequences of a breakthrough. The 1974 Pokhran 'peaceful nuclear explosion' ought to have, in rapid succession, been followed up by more, rather than waiting until 1998 for another PM to find the resolve to go forward with another round of tests. After the Pokhran tests, there was a flurry of interest in India that, for some time, was reflected even in the growth of exports of manufacturing—a country that could make a nuclear bomb could be depended upon to make the lathe. However, even Vajpayee declined to follow up on Pokhran II. There was a moratorium on further tests, and India locked itself within most of the bounds of the Treaty on the Non-Proliferation of Nuclear Weapons although it was not a binding document.

Avoiding risk and looking for the soft option has been the cause of much of the pain that India and its people have endured as a consequence of defective (or at best inadequate) policy structures. Ensuring that the country gets the worst rather than the best of both worlds has become an art form in the Lutyens Zone. The 75th anniversary of Indian independence has brought with it another opportunity for the country to propel itself forward and escape from the suboptimal achievement levels that it continues to be mired in. In a smart world, smart policy is needed, and citizens look to such an unprecedented situation with hope. If the chance for a generation of rapid economic growth, and the benefits this brings, is cast away, historians in India might forgive those who are in power. History will not.

Acknowledgements

I am grateful to Dr Dhanasree Jayaram of the Department of Geopolitics and International Relations, Manipal Academy of Higher Education, for helping in the presentation of the concepts in this book.

I would also like to thank Ms Poornima B. of the Department of Geopolitics and International Relations, Manipal Academy of Higher Education, for her assistance in contextualizing several events presented in this book.

Notes

FOREWORD

1 'India Needs to Revisit 1962 Humiliation for Catharsis', *The Times of India*, 10 October 2012, https://bit.ly/3M2YgRw. Accessed on 30 May 2022.

INTRODUCTION

1 Seymour, Margaret, 'The Problem with Soft Power', Foreign Policy Research Institute, 14 September 2020, https://bit.ly/3t0rvOg. Accessed on 30 May 2022.
2 'Comparing China and India by Economy', Statistics Times, 16 May 2021, https://bit.ly/3avCLMi. Accessed on 30 May 2022.

CHAPTER 1: AN INHERITANCE SYSTEMATICALLY DRAINED OF SUBSTANCE

1 Judging by the measures taken post-1947 to ignore essential Hindu demands such as freedom of temples from state control, it was as though the Partition had never happened.
2 Nalapat, M.D., 'The Case for India-Alignment', Gateway House, 24 September 2013, https://bit.ly/3awmZRj. Accessed on 31 May 2022.
3 Walker, Tony, '"To Get Rich Is Glorious": How Deng Xiaoping Set China on a Path to Rule the World', *The Conversation*, 9 July 2021, https://bit.ly/3qO7mtB. Accessed on 30 March 2022.
4 Matthews, Roderick, *Jinnah vs. Gandhi*, Hachette India, 2014.
5 Roy, Haimanti, *The Partition of India*, OUP, Oxford, 2018; Boissoneault, Lorraine, 'The Genocide the U.S. Can't Remember, But Bangladesh

Can't Forget', *Smithsonian Magazine*, 16 December 2016, https://bit.ly/3NxRkgA. Accessed on 24 May 2022.

6 'Muslim Population by Country 2022', World Population Review, https://bit.ly/3Nr19gJ. Accessed on 31 March 2022.

7 Ibid.

8 Lentin, Sifra, 'UK's Irregular Indians: Colonial Carry-Over', Gateway House, 2 June 2021, https://bit.ly/3GasdOt. Accessed on 24 May 2022; 'Voices: Our Untold Stories', *BBC*, https://bbc.in/3LGaUpz. Accessed on 24 May 2022.

9 Anand, Dibyesh, '1962 India-China War: Wrong Lessons', *The Economic Times*, 22 March 2014, https://bit.ly/3MBg33r. Accessed on 24 May 2022.

10 Rajadhyaksha, Niranjan, 'Opinion | Lessons for India from Other Economies in the Asian Region', *Mint*, 15 January 2020, https://bit.ly/3sd4vuY. Accessed on 5 May 2022.

11 Yew, Lee Kwan, 'Singapore's Lee Kuan Yew on Why He Departed from Nehruvian Welfarism', *The Scroll*, 23 March 2015, https://bit.ly/3w8vyJ1. Accessed on 6 May 2022.

CHAPTER 2: THE RISE OF CHINA AND COLD WAR 2.0

1 Wyne, Ali, 'Beware a "New Cold War" Narrative for the U.S. and China', *Fortune*, 1 February 2022, https://bit.ly/3KEWaGY. Accessed on 5 May 2022; Christensen, Thomas J., 'No New Cold War: Why US-China Strategic Competition Will Not Be like the US-Soviet Cold War', Asan Institute for Policy Studies, 2020. http://www.jstor.org/stable/resrep26078. Accessed on 30 May 2022.

2 'China's Rich Lists Riddled with Communist Party Members', *Forbes*, 14 September 2011, https://bit.ly/3MZ1WoX. Accessed on 30 May 2022.

3 Chan, Sylvia, 'The Image of a "Capitalist Roader"—Some Dissident Short Stories in the Hundred Flowers Period', *The Australian Journal of Chinese Affairs*, Vol. 2, July 1979, https://bit.ly/3r6mJ0L. Accessed on 6 April 2022.

4 Coble, Parks M., '"Is China Going Capitalist?" The Debate Over Admitting Private Entrepreneurs to Membership in the Chinese Communist Party', *Studies on Asia 2004*, Vol. 3 No. 2, pp. 20–27, https://bit.ly/3tXIwcL. Accessed on 1 April 2022.

5 Li, Mark Z., *The People's Republic of China, 1949-2012: A Political Economy Perspective*, 2013, George Mason University, PhD dissertation, pp. 54–55. https://bit.ly/37g9F23. Accessed on 5 May 2022.

6 'What Does "Path of Socialism with Chinese Characteristics" Mean?', *CGTN*, https://bit.ly/3zaF2qm. Accessed on 30 May 2022.

7 '"Full Text" of Top-Secret Fourth Plenary Session Document: Li Peng's Life-Taking Report Lays Blame on Zhao Ziyang', *Chinese Law & Government*, Vol. 38, No. 3, 2005, 7 December 2014, https://doi.org/10.1080/00094609.2005.11036459. Accessed on 30 May 2022.

8 Simes, Dimitri, 'China and Russia Ditch Dollar in Move towards "Financial Alliance"', *Financial Times*, 17 August 2020, https://on.ft.com/3DKj1Pw. Accessed on 6 April 2022.

9 Childs, Nick, 'China's Carrier-Aviation Developments: Making a Difference', *IIS: Military Balance Blog*, 3 June 2018, https://bit.ly/3KhvaOh. Accessed on 6 April 2022.

10 Dangwal, Ashish, 'Xi Jinping's Top Advisor Says China Can Launch Invasion of Taiwan by 2027, Restrict US Navy Within 1,000 Nautical Miles', *The EurAsian Times*, 31 January 2022, https://bit.ly/3vKMIO8. Accessed on 5 May 2022.

11 'Beijing Tells NATO to Stop Hyping Up China Threat', *BBC*, 15 June 2021, https://bbc.in/3GBApHO. Accessed on 31 May 2022.

12 'EU-China Relations: Smoke, Mirrors and Reality', Institut Montaigne, 2 September 2020, https://bit.ly/3lTM2QK. Accessed on 31 May 2022.

13 Phillips, Tom, 'Xi Jinping Heralds "New Era" of Chinese Power at Communist Party Congress', *The Guardian*, 18 October 2017, https://bit.ly/39FABt1. Accessed on 5 May 2022.

14 Almén, Oscar, 'The Chinese Communist Party and the Diaspora: Beijing's Extraterritorial Authoritarian Rule', FOI, March 2020, https://bit.ly/3M3mE5J. Accessed on 31 May 2022.

15 'Permanent Suspension of @realDonaldTrump', Twitter Blog, 8 January 2021, https://bit.ly/3s5AcGC. Accessed on 2 May 2022.

16 Evans, Zachary, 'Canada Unlocks "Vast Majority" of Bank Accounts Frozen over Support for Trucker Convoy', *National Review*, 23 February 2022, https://bit.ly/3s60NDj. Accessed on 2 May 2022.

17 Lakshman, Sriram, 'Biden Releases Proposal to Seize Russian Oligarchs' U.S. Assets and Give to Ukraine', *The Hindu*, 29 April 2022, https://bit.ly/3axzoo7. Accessed on 31 May 2022.

18 'China Wants to Form Its Own Military Alliance', YouTube, https://youtu.be/ujeBkrQ1z0o. Accessed on 31 May 2022.

19 Succimarra, Guiseppe, 'The Last "Legal" Threat against Uyghurs: China and Turkey Ratified the Extradition Treaty', Human Rights Pulse, 26 January 2021, https://bit.ly/3uQhN12. Accessed on 4 April 2022.

20 Fraser, Suzan, 'AP Explains: What Lies behind Turkish Support for

Azerbaijan', *AP News*, 2 October 2020, https://bit.ly/3K6gyRH. Accessed on 4 April 2022.

21 Nalapat, M.D., 'PLA Ally GHQ Rawalpindi's Terror Toolkit Makes Deadly Progress', *The Sunday Guardian Live*, 27 December 2020, https://bit.ly/3vY6xjO. Accessed on 5 May 2022.

22 He, Di, 'The Most Respected Enemy: Mao Zedong's Perception of the United States', *The China Quarterly*, No. 137, 1994, pp. 144–158. *JSTOR*, http://www.jstor.org/stable/655690. Accessed on 31 May 2022.

23 Sing, Lam Lai, *Conservatism and the Kissinger-Mao Axis: Development of the Twin Global Orders*, Lexington Books, 2015, p. 49.

24 Dasgupta, Chandrashekhar, 'The 1971 War: When Richard Nixon and Henry Kissinger Failed to "Scare Off" the Indians', *FirstPost*, 10 December 2021, https://bit.ly/3lV0DLF. Accessed on 31 May 2022; Brands, Hal, *What Good Is Grand Strategy?: Power and Purpose in American Statecraft from Harry S. Truman to George W. Bush*, Cornell University Press, 2014; Chang, Gordon G., 'Taiwan: "The Struggle Continues"', Strategika, No. 65, 29 May 2020, https://hvr.co/3NNfxiP. Accessed on 31 May 2022.

25 Choi, Joseph, 'Documents Show Chinese Government Collects Droves of Data from Western Social Media: Report', *The Hill*, 31 December 2021, https://bit.ly/3Fk4tqo. Accessed on 5 May 2022.

26 Rogin, Josh, 'Opinion | Biden Doesn't Want to Change China. He Wants to Beat It', *The Washington Post*, 10 February 2022, https://wapo.st/3kIraeC. Accessed on 5 May 2022.

27 Kamal, Kajari and Gokul Sahni, 'India in the Indo-Pacific: A Kautilyan Strategy for the Maritime Mandala', ORF Issue Brief, 21 February 2022, https://bit.ly/3abfJKc. Accessed on 31 May 2022.

28 'Xi Focus: Building a Peace-Loving World-Class Military', *Xinhuanet*, 1 August 2021, https://bit.ly/3ycGng5. Accessed on 2 May 2022.

CHAPTER 3: AN INEVITABLE CLASH OF OPPOSING SYSTEMS

1 Mourdoukoutas, Panos, 'Time for the Chinese Communist Party To Drop "Communist" From Its Name', *Forbes*, 17 December 2017, https://bit.ly/3yiEjDc. Accessed on 9 May 2022.

2 Similarly, in an earlier era, some of the communist parties in Europe were named 'Eurocommunists' to distinguish them from their counterparts in Eastern Europe.

3 'Targeted by US, China Has to Do Three Things: Global Times Editorial',

Global Times, 15 April 2021, https://bit.ly/3MGyB1V. Accessed on 2 May 2022.

4 'China: Possible Missile Technology Transfers Under U.S. Satellite Export Policy—Actions and Chronology', EveryCRSReport.com, 6 October 2003, https://bit.ly/3w8mfJh. Accessed on 5 May 2022.

5 Kuran, Timur, 'Now Out of Never: The Element of Surprise in the East European Revolution of 1989', *World Politics*, Vol. 44, No. 1, October 1991, pp. 7–48, https://doi.org/10.2307/2010422. Accessed on 31 May 2022.

6 Meisels, A. Greer, 'What China Learned from the USSR's Fall', *The Diplomat*, 27 July 2012, https://bit.ly/3KpCrvK. Accessed on 7 April 2022.

7 Dikötter, Frank, *Mao's Great Famine: The History of China's Most Devastating Catastrophe, 1958-1962*, Bloomsbury Paperbacks, 2018.

CHAPTER 4: THE INDISPENSABLE INDO-PACIFIC PARTNER

1 Heath, Timothy R., Derek Grossman, Asha Clark, 'China's Quest for Global Primacy', RAND Corporation, 2021, https://bit.ly/3x0IAbV. Accessed on 31 May 2022.

2 Bernstein, Andrea, 'Where Trump Learned the Art of the Quid Pro Quo', *The Atlantic*, 20 January 2020, https://bit.ly/37jJzeh. Accessed on 7 April 2022.

3 'India Is Cutting Back Its Reliance on Russian Arms', *The Economist*, 14 April 2022, https://econ.st/3FvNd1C. Accessed on 10 May 2022.

4 Nalapat, M.D., 'Western Media Stands by Two-Nation Theory', *The Sunday Guardian Live*, 10 August 2019, https://bit.ly/3OVnl3A. Accessed on 5 May 2022; Gould, Harold A., 'Bill Clinton's Moribund South Asia Policy', *Economic and Political Weekly*, Vol. 31, No. 47, November 1996, pp. 3078–3084, https://www.jstor.org/stable/4404801. Accessed on 31 May 2022.

5 Cohen, Edy, Dr, 'A Short History of Palestinian Rejectionism', The Begin-Sadat Center for Strategic Studies, 16 February 2020, https://bit.ly/384awDv. Accessed on 5 May 2022.

6 Ranjan, Prabhash, 'Use International Law, Call Out China's Violations', *The Hindu*, 22 February 2022, https://bit.ly/3NEImOQ. Accessed on 8 June 2022.

7 Bedi, Rahul, 'Chinese Pullback at Galwan Comes at a Cost, Indian Retreat Shifts LAC to Its Disadvantage', *The Wire*, 9 July 2020, https://bit.ly/3yw3Xof. Accessed on 5 May 2022.

8 Gould, Harold A., 'Bill Clinton's Moribund South Asia Policy', *Economic*

and Political Weekly, Vol. 31, No. 47, November 1996, pp. 3078–3084, https://www.jstor.org/stable/4404801. Accessed on 31 May 2022; Nalapat, M.D., 'Pakistan Army Veto Hurts India-China Interests (Sunday Guardian)', The Writings of M D Nalapat, 19 May 2013, https://bit.ly/3PQRp0U. Accessed on 31 May 2022.

9 Coll, Steve, 'The Back Channel', *The New Yorker*, 22 February 2022, https://bit.ly/3t1t2Us. Accessed on 30 May 2022; 'Back Channel: The Promise and Peril', Ministry of External Affairs, Government of India, 20 May 2003, https://bit.ly/3GtC4Px. Accessed on 30 May 2022.

10 Balakrishnan, Uday, 'A Lost Opportunity in 1971: Where Indira Gandhi Erred', *The Hindu*, 20 November 2019, https://bit.ly/3xiLzhG. Accessed on 11 April 2022.

11 Chandra, Nirmal Kumar, 'India's Rouble Debt and Depreciating Rouble', *Economic and Political Weekly*, Vol. 28, No. 27/28, July 1993, pp. 1443–1452, https://bit.ly/37ykLzh. Accessed on 11 April 2022.

12 Braw, Elisabeth, 'The Geopolitics of Video Games', *Foreign Policy Magazine*, 24 December 2021, https://bit.ly/3rdaDTp. Accessed on 11 April 2022.

13 Cadell, Cate, 'China Harvests Masses of Data on Western Targets, Documents Show', *The Washington Post*, 31 December 2021, https://wapo.st/3v90cBB. Accessed on 11 April 2022.

14 Balding, Christopher, 'China's Collection of Data on Foreigners Is a National Security Risk', *Discourse*, 29 November 2021, https://bit.ly/3utIyt7. Accessed on 11 April 2022.

15 This information is based on the author's personal conversations with officials.

16 'India and the United States: Partners in the Fight Against HIV/AIDS', Ministry of External Affairs, 18 July 2005, https://bit.ly/3xgCkys. Accessed on 5 May 2022.

17 Varma, K.J.M., 'China Backs Pakistan on Kashmir, Opposes Unilateral Action by India, Says Resolve Dispute Peacefully', *The Print*, 21 August 2020, https://bit.ly/3EaEjWR. Accessed on 14 April 2022.

18 Chappell, Bill, 'Turkey Accepts Russian S-400 Missile System, Rankling U.S. And NATO', *NPR*, 12 July 2019, https://n.pr/3MeaeIm. Accessed on 14 April 2022.

19 'Prof M D Nalapat on the Impending Us Sanctions on India on S-400 and How India Should Respond', YouTube, https://youtu.be/P_7Avoq59FY. Accessed on 31 May 2022.

CHAPTER 5: OPPORTUNITY KNOCKS TWICE AT INDIA'S DOOR

1 Aiyar, Swaminathan S. Anklesaria, 'Ill-Informed Debate on Oil Decontrol,' *The Economic Times,* 30 June 2010, https://bit.ly/38xkSvZ. Accessed on 31 May 2022; Nalapat, M.D., 'Lessons from 1969 Congress Politics Then and Now,' The Writings of M D Nalapat, 2 January 1999, https://bit.ly/3z3yx8R. Accessed on 31 May 2022.

2 In 2020, a similarly tiny window of time was given before a complete lockdown was imposed on the entire country in order to limit the spread of Covid-19.

3 '99.30% Of Demonetised Money Back in the System, Says RBI Report,' *The Economic Times,* 30 August 2018, https://bit.ly/3MFPwS8. Accessed on 2 May 2022.

4 Mathew, Ashlin, 'Did Modi Govt Exchange Fake Currency during Demonetisation? RBI Report Says So,' *National Herald,* 4 February 2019, https://bit.ly/3kISRnr. Accessed on 5 May 2022.

5 Chase, Allison, 'Fed's Counterfeiting Experts Fight Flow of Fake Money,' Federal Reserve Bank of Boston, 15 October 2019, https://bit.ly/3F4wAKm. Accessed on 2 May 2022.

6 Kishore, Roshan, 'Five Years since Demonetisation: What Has Changed?,' *Hindustan Times,* 8 November 2021, https://bit.ly/3vX5fpl. Accessed on 2 May 2022.

7 Rowlatt, Justin, 'Why India Wiped Out 86% Of Its Cash Overnight,' *BBC,* 14 November 2016, https://bbc.in/3uVLXRZ. Accessed on 19 April 2022.

8 Ray, Atmadip, 'RBI Governor Urjit Patel Says Demonetisation Was Well Planned,' *The Economic Times,* https://bit.ly/3857E9a. Accessed on 19 April 2022.

9 Chandak, Bhawarlal, 'Why We Are in the Midst of a Liquidity Crisis,' *BusinessLine,* 17 September 2019, https://bit.ly/3vxagEV. Accessed on 19 April 2022.

10 'GST: Indian System among the Most Complex Globally, Says World Bank Report,' *Business Standard,* 16 March 2018, https://bit.ly/3vZxbKl. Accessed on 10 May 2022.

11 'Why Are Foreign Tech Firms Pulling Out of China?,' *The Economic Times,* 3 November 2021, https://bit.ly/3KZ4MJl. Accessed on 19 April 2022.

12 'TSMC, UMC May Set Up Semiconductor Chip Manufacturing Plant as India, Taiwan Look to Firm Up Free-Trade Pact,' *Swarajya,* 20 December 2021, https://bit.ly/3vwpmeX. Accessed on 2 May 2022.

13 Kosowatz, John, 'Is There an Alternative to China?,' *ASME: Mechanical Engineering Magazine,* Vol. 142, No. 9, pp. 30–35, https://doi.

org/10.1115/1.2020-SEP1. Accessed on 3 June 2022.

14 'Creating a Conducive Business Environment - Modi 2.0's Mantra,' NarendraModi.in, 27 May 2020, https://bit.ly/3FuIYn3. Accessed on 10 May 2022.

15 'India Hopes "Pharma City" Hyderabad Will Break China's Grip on the Industry,' *Mint*, 12 April 2022, https://bit.ly/3ErndE4. Accessed on 19 April 2022.

16 Nalapat, M.D., '$1 Trillion External Investment Awaits Modi 2.0 Policy Matrix,' *The Sunday Guardian Live*, 8 June 2019, https://bit.ly/3a7QJng. Accessed on 31 May 2022.

17 Nalapat, M.D., 'Importance of Indutva - Moderation Is the Key to Harmony,' *The Times of India*, 21 January 1998.

18 Dutta, Amrita Nayak, 'Govt Opens Door to Private Sector Talent, Wants Specialists to Join Ministries as Joint Secys,' 10 June 2018, *The Print*, https://bit.ly/3ErfSUZ. Accessed on 19 April 2022.

19 'Supreme Court of India: Prakash Singh & Ors vs Union of India and Ors on 22 September, 2006,' IndianKanoon, https://bit.ly/3z6NdnQ. Accessed on 30 May 2022; Nalapat, M.D., 'PM Modi Has Entrusted Reform to IAS, IPS, IFS,' *The Sunday Guardian Live*, 15 December 2018, https://bit.ly/3a7YCJh. Accessed on 30 May 2022.

20 Nalapat, M.D., 'Euro-Atlantic Quad Takes Shape under Macron,' *The Sunday Guardian Live*, 27 February 2021, https://bit.ly/3N6TiEW. Accessed on 31 May 2022.

21 McCubbing, Gus, 'Scott Morrison Continues Calls for Investigation into Origins of Covid-19,' 25 September 2021, *7News*, https://bit.ly/3tlUP1S. Accessed on 9 June 2022.

22 Nalapat, M.D., 'Netanyahu Hints at Path India Must Take,' *The Sunday Guardian Live*, 20 January 2018, https://bit.ly/3kIwpei. Accessed on 5 May 2022.

CHAPTER 6: INDIA'S 'NEAR ABROAD'

1 'India-China Trade on Course to Touch Record $100 Billion-Mark,' *India Today*, 13 October 2021, https://bit.ly/3Fgie9L. Accessed on 5 May 2022.

2 Iyer, Vaidyanathan P. and Jay Mazoomdaar, 'Explained: Why China Harvests India Data, Why Track Public Figures,' *The Indian Express*, 18 September 2020, https://bit.ly/3rFNDgk. Accessed on 21 April 2022.

3 Nalapat, M.D., 'Whose Truth? (Far Eastern Economic Review),' The Writings of M D Nalapat, 2 September 2004, https://bit.ly/3MI1OcB. Accessed on 2 May 2022.

4 This was shared with the author in a private conversation with an insistence on anonymity.

5 This was shared with the author in a private conversation.

6 'Xiaomi and 8 Other Chinese Companies Blacklisted by the US over Alleged Military Links,' *Tech2*, 2 February 2021, https://bit.ly/3whNeSH. Accessed on 10 May 2022.

7 'Muslim Population by Country 2022,' World Population Review, https://bit.ly/3EszfwU. Accessed on 20 April 2022.

8 'US Sanctions on Iran Have No Bearing on India's Chabahar Port Project: Govt,' *Business Standard*, 10 December 2021, https://bit.ly/3N2wfLr. Accessed on 31 May 2022.

9 'India Stopped Importing Iranian Oil after Us Waiver Expired: Envoy,' *Business Today*, 24 May 2019, https://bit.ly/3w40L00. Accessed on 5 May 2022.

10 Ottaway, David, 'Will Saudi Arabia's Social Revolution Provoke a Wahhabi Backlash?,' Wilson Center, https://bit.ly/384ds2Z. Accessed on 5 May 2022.

CHAPTER 7: INDIA IN ITS IMMEDIATE NEIGHBOURHOOD

1 'What Is the Most Blatant Lie Taught through Pakistan Textbooks?,' *Dawn*, 15 August 2014, https://bit.ly/3k6rxPM. Accessed on 25 April 2022.

2 Zaidi, Akbar, S., 'South Asia? West Asia? Pakistan: Location, Identity,' *The Economic and Political Weekly*, Vol. 44, No. 10, 7 March 2007, https://bit.ly/3Om1yRJ. Accessed on 9 June 2022.

3 Nalapat, M.D., 'Pak GHQ Using PLA "Neocons" to Damage India-China Ties,' *The Sunday Guardian Live*, 13 August 2017, https://bit.ly/3wSqjxA. Accessed on 31 May 2022.

4 Tiwari, Gopal, 'Gandhi's Last Protest: How He Blackmailed India into Giving 55 Cr to Pakistan, Dragged Hindu, Sikh Refugees Seeking Shelter in Mosques to Die in Cold,' *OpIndia*, 14 January 2022, https://bit.ly/3vcqrIF. Accessed on 25 April 2022.

5 'Why I Killed Gandhi: Godse's Final Address,' *The Free Press Journal*, 29 May 2019, https://bit.ly/3kbivks. Accessed on 25 April 2022.

6 Mishra, Anshuman, 'Bilateral Trade between India and China Crosses USD 90 Billion in First Three Quarters of 2021,' *DD News*, 14 October 2021, https://bit.ly/3yc5L5z. Accessed on 5 May 2022.

7 Waghmare, Abhishek and Subhayan Chakraborty, 'How Chinese Goods

Are Choking Indian Industry and Economy: The Hard Numbers,' *Business Standard*, 28 July 2018, https://bit.ly/3OCxWA8. Accessed on 25 April 2022.

8 Mohanty, Prasanna, 'Why India's Manufacturing Dependence on China Continues to Grow,' *Fortune India*, 9 February 2022, https://bit.ly/3vJdFkZ. Accessed on 5 May 2022; 'Five Indian Companies with Big China Exposure,' *Mint*, 6 August 2021, https://bit.ly/3KL7gtW. Accessed on 5 May 2022.

9 Khatlani, Sameer Arshad, 'In Fact: Punjabis Dominate the Pakistan Army — But Only Just,' *The Indian Express*, 7 December 2016, https://bit.ly/36HzMPa. Accessed on 25 April 2022.

10 '"Don't Understand Why": Bangladesh PM on India's Amended Citizenship Law,' *The Hindustan Times*, 28 August 2020, https://bit.ly/3k6AV60. Accessed on 25 April 2022.

11 'Crisis of Impunity: Pakistan's Support of the Taliban,' Human Rights Watch, https://bit.ly/3wqghUm. Accessed on 11 May 2022.

CHAPTER 8: HARD CHOICES, NEVER SOFT OPTIONS

1 Nalapat, M.D., 'India's 5,000-Year Legacy Leaves Lifestyles Alone,' *The Sunday Guardian Live*, 11 March 2016, https://bit.ly/3M4b1Lz. Accessed on 30 May 2022.

2 'Karnataka Hijab Row Highlights: Muslim Girls Booked, Suspended from Colleges for Wearing Hijab, Holding Protest,' *The Indian Express*, 20 February 2022, https://bit.ly/3MVNL3M. Accessed on 30 May 2022.

3 '"Denounce What India Is Doing to Kashmiris": Canadian MP Jagmeet Singh,' *Outlook*, 30 September 2019, https://bit.ly/3vKWKig. Accessed on 5 May 2022.

4 Som, Vishnu, '"Expansionism Shows Distorted Mindset": PM Slams China in Diwali Speech,' *NDTV*, 15 November 2015, https://bit.ly/3EHz016. Accessed on 25 April 2022.

5 Gonzalez, Jenipher Camino, 'Venezuela and the US: From friends to Foes,' DW, 25 January 2019, https://bit.ly/3ynbCVs. Accessed on 5 May 2022.

Index